FINDING FREEDOM IN A FRAMEWORK

MOVING OUT OF CHAOS AND INTO PURPOSE

FINDING FREEDOM IN A FRAMEWORK

MOVING OUT OF CHAOS AND INTO PURPOSE

By
Michelle Hubert

Publishing Services by Happy Self Publishing
www.happyselfpublishing.com

Year: 2018

TABLE OF CONTENTS

The presence of a framework invites more moments of freedom than chaos.

The absence of a framework creates more moments in chaos than freedom.

INTRODUCTION:
WHY FREEDOM?

Have you had moments of your life when you've felt completely at peace? When it appears as if all is well, and everything is on the right track with your life? Have you also had moments when you have felt as if the world was crashing down on you? Or that you were living in utter chaos?

How do we find ourselves in perfect peace (or freedom) or in chaos at different points in our lives? Do we invite the chaos, or does it just show up? In moments of complete freedom, is it just pure luck?

Why do we need a framework?

"Successful and unsuccessful people
do not vary greatly in their abilities.
They vary in their desires to reach their
potential."
— John C. Maxwell

The intensity of our desire for success drives our daily decision making. The reality is that the only difference between successful and unsuccessful people is what they do with their 12 hours. We all have the same 24 hours a day to design success. We can spend the second 12 hours on sleep and recharging, but our success or failure depends on how we choose to spend the first 12 hours of the day. Whether or not we're successful is not dependent on our background, education, economic status, geography, intelligence, or any other factor. It is how we spend our time, and no one has any more than anyone else. It's our most precious commodity and needs to be treated as such. It's the daily choices we make and the habits we create compounded over time that determine our success or failure.

That realization was life-changing for me, and it shifted the trajectory of my career in a huge way. When I started designing a framework for how to maximize my 12 hours, I went from a struggling entrepreneur to moving into the top 10% in my industry. It didn't happen overnight, but changing my daily decisions and habits were all that was needed to change course. I was able to generate very different results in the same market with the same products. The only difference was the framework. The reality is that we're perfectly aligned to get the result we're currently getting. If we want a different result, we need to start making different daily decisions.

I often speak about moving from surviving to thriving. I discuss how having the right framework in place can help us reduce chaos and work from a proactive perspective rather than a reactive one. Reading the 2011 book titled *Traction: Get a Grip on Your Business* by Gino Wickman created another life-changing moment for me. It was in reviewing the similarities between my business operating system and EOS – the Entrepreneurial Operating System that Gino outlines in his book — that I made a discovery: I realized having a framework personally, spiritually, and for my family was just as important as having one professionally. If we create the right framework, we can create high levels of success for ourselves, and in the organizations we serve.

It may seem at times that someone has it all together. There have been times my life has appeared that way. People see someone who is organized and driven. From the outside looking in, everything looks picture perfect. There are times I feel that peace, and I live in the freedom of it. There have also been times I have thought to myself, "I'm glad it looks that way to you on the outside because all I'm feeling on the inside is chaos." Maybe you've felt that before too? It looks like you have it all together on the outside, living the "perfect life," but you feel it could all come crashing down any moment? If we have moments of freedom, how do we multiply those moments and exist in that space consistently? Is it about peace? Is it about our beliefs? Is it about managing our time better? Freedom is found in the framework we live in, and this book will help you design the life you deserve...the one that facilitates an abundance of freedom and removes chaos from your life.

> "Freedom is not about the size of your cage, or the power of your wings, or nonattachment to a person or a thing. Freedom is about being so truly, madly, and deeply attached to your own soul that you can't bear—if only for a moment—a life that doesn't honor it."
>
> —Andrea Balt

I *love* that quote, and I feel the truth of it deep in my soul. It affirms there is Freedom in the Framework. Being "attached to your own soul" speaks to authenticity. Our journey to freedom is predicated on our ability to live in pure authenticity, which is easier said than done. The world—and more intimately, our circle of influence—is always trying to convince us of what we should think, how we should act, and who we should be. Isn't it true that most of the people around us teach us *what* to think rather than *how* to think?

It's very difficult, and at the same time, vitally necessary, we find a way to shut out the noise so we can connect with the very best, most authentic parts of who we are. Making our way to true authenticity is a journey that often starts with the work of *connecting* with our most authentic selves. After we find clarity, we can then move toward embracing who we are. Acknowledging we are each unique for a reason. Our journey should be focused on fully surrendering to who we are and coming into alignment with our personal path.

The best gift of surrender, and resulting freedom, is that it moves us away from comparison—trying to be someone or something we aren't. It's exhausting and keeps us from all that the universe has in store for us. It's the opposite of what we think, we win by being the most authentic version of ourselves rather than trying to imitate someone else. It's about being vulnerable enough to let the world experience who we really are. Only then are we able deliver our unique gifts and stand out in a way that only we can. No one can beat you at being you.

The second part of the quote reaffirms there's Freedom in a Framework. "Freedom is about being so truly, madly, and deeply attached to your own soul that you can't bear—if only for a moment—a life that doesn't honor it." You can't bear to live a life without it, so you MUST build a framework that supports honoring your soul. Your unique, individual soul.

What's onerous—a burden, or troublesome—is living in chaos, which is often the result of living our lives without guidelines, boundaries, or a framework. When we establish a strong foundation or framework, it sets us free to fully live in who we are, our personal values, and to fulfill our purpose. It allows us to limit the chaos, distractions, and obstacles that can derail our plans, hinder our progress, and hold us back from achieving our full potential. It bridges the gap between what we know and what we do. We were *all* created for a life of significance, not survival. It's only when we create and live within a solid framework that we can fully step into significance.

True freedom also comes from boundaries. Boundaries release us to do our best work, be our best selves, and bring our highest level of creativity to whatever problem we're trying to solve. It's important to know that we can say no, and in fact, we should be saying no a lot more often than we do. When we know our values, decisions become easy. With boundaries in place and our values clear, it's easier to say no to something that either takes us away from our values or doesn't move us closer to our purpose. People who know who they are, what they stand for, and where they're headed, have no problem saying no to people and things that don't align with their purpose.

What makes people successful has nothing to do with the fact that they're smarter or more talented than anyone else. They are successful because they have discovered their unique abilities and have built a framework around leveraging them every day. They develop daily habits, set boundaries, and pursue growth in a way that feeds into those abilities. It's most visible in professional athletes. They build and live in a framework which allows them to perform at levels others don't. They invest in themselves in a way that allows them to be able to deliver their gift to the world. We all have a gift within us. Most people go through life either fighting it or failing to discover or develop it.

As a business owner and coach for the last 28 years, I've found most businesses are operating in chaos daily. They are succeeding in spite of themselves. They spend their days reacting to what is coming at them, with no time or energy left for proactively moving their business, family, or themselves forward. There are more items on their to-do list than will ever get done. Their email inbox is out of control, and they feel like they are prisoners to their phone. They dream of a day when their businesses and lives will be better organized and running like a well-oiled machine. I know what that looks and feels like because I've lived in that chaos. I've also lived in freedom. That freedom was born out of a framework that I've created over the last 20 years. It's why I wrote this book and what I want to share with you. Creating a framework can set us free to be our very best, contribute at a much higher level, AND increase our quality of life.

What keeps us from freedom?

When we evaluate our success personally or professionally, it's just as important that we consider what we need to stop doing. What are those things that aren't moving us forward? What is keeping us stuck?

We need to stop:

- Living according to someone else's values
- Comparing ourselves to others
- Reinventing the wheel – "working harder"

- Relying on someone else to develop us or drive our growth
- Making decisions based on fear
- Focusing on what we're receiving rather than what we're contributing

Successful people live fully in their personal values, owning their authenticity. They leverage daily habits to keep them focused in the right direction and never put their development in someone else's hands. They are bold and courageous and make decisions regardless of fear – evaluating potential risk and reward. They look for the growth opportunity and stay focused on what they can contribute to others.

Our personal and professional lives are intimately intertwined. It makes sense to apply some of the same principles that lead to success in business to our personal lives. This book can do that for you. It explains how to build and live within a framework that can deliver freedom from chaos, obstacles, challenges, barriers, and plateaus. Just as a strong operating system can help us succeed professionally, the same is true for our families. It's time to stop settling for what life is "giving" us and start designing the life we deserve.

Once you build and live in a framework, it can set you free to make the most of your unique abilities and position you to deliver what only you can to the world. By creating this framework now, we can all work to build a legacy of freedom for our business partners, but more importantly, for our families.

In our daily lives, we are operating either by default or by design. Either we are trying to survive because we don't have a structure to operate within, or we're operating by design and taking care of our most important priorities first, according to a well-thought-out plan. *Operating by design* also means when issues arise—and they always will—we have a plan to lean on that can support us and help us move past a challenge or a plateau. We can evaluate strategies and results and make smart adjustments as needed. With a framework in place, we are operating by design, moving toward the life we want to live.

You've seen it

You know what freedom looks like when you see it. There are a few high-profile people who come to mind. Oprah Winfrey is one of them. She's a successful media proprietor, talk show host, actress, producer, and philanthropist. She suffered plenty of struggles and setbacks early in life. What has led to her overwhelming success? Did she "get lucky?" No, she has spent a lifetime designing a framework to operate in. One that supports her living to her personal values. Moving her deeper into true authenticity. Creating the right daily habits and decisions. Ensuring she's learning and growing and living FULLY in her purpose. As a result, she's building a legacy true to who she is and what she wants to contribute to the world. That doesn't happen by accident, it's by design.

Kari Jobe is another one who comes to mind. If you're not familiar, she's a contemporary Christian music singer and songwriter. If you've ever seen her perform, there is an air of authenticity around her that is so rare. Often, performers of any kind have a stage presence or persona that keeps them from fully revealing themselves to us. With Kari, you can sense and feel that she's gifting the very best and most authentic version of herself. You can tell she's living a life of freedom.

One final example would be Steve Harvey. Is it by luck that Steve is involved in so many successful projects? He's a successful comedian, television host, producer, radio personality, actor, and author. When you experience Steve in any of those arenas, you experience him fully. Sometimes people say it this way: "What you see is what you get." I can only assume all of his success is a result of him living within a framework that keeps him in his values, focused on the right things daily, and delivering his unique gifts to the world in a way that's building a legacy.

Do these people lead perfect lives? Of course not. We are all human. We're going to stumble from time to time. We're going to take a bad risk or make a bad decision. The question is, do we have a framework we live within that puts us right back on track, extracting the lesson, and moving us forward smarter and stronger than before?

You know some "free" people in your personal circle. I know some as well, and they are "my people." They are the people I want to be around and be influenced by – because I know they will help me along in my freedom journey. Encouraging me to be true to myself, make good decisions, and focus on delivering my unique gift to the world. From business partners to a dear, sweet lady from my church…you know it when you're around them. They make you feel more grounded, more confident in embracing who you are, and encourage you to be obedient to what the world is calling you to contribute.

3 Key Components of Freedom

My personal mission statement is to live a life that's balanced, organized, and structured in such a way that I can spend most of my time helping others. It's what led me to this framework for freedom.

It starts with embracing who we are by clarifying personal values and living authentically. Then we can move on to designing our lives. Leveraging habits to drive the right daily decisions and aggressively pursuing growth.

Finally, it's living fully in purpose and utilizing our framework to be of service to others – building our legacy. Embrace YOU. Design Your Life. Build Your Legacy. That's the framework!

For me, freedom is about being able to *fully* live into that—to create a framework that sets me free to be of service to others. I'm happiest and at my very best—and believe I am fully delivering my unique talents and abilities to the world—when I'm serving others. It took me a very long time to come to that realization. It's always been in me, I just had to go through a process to uncover and crystallize it so I could begin to move toward it every day. Part of my purpose is to help you build a framework that creates more freedom in your life – and there are 4 key areas we can focus on.

4 Areas for Freedom

At different times or seasons in their lives, most people feel like they've "got it all together" in a particular area. It's rare, though, to find people who would attest to operating at a very high level in all 4 areas at the same time. Why are some people able to achieve that on a consistent basis? Is it luck? Good genetics? A great education? The right mentor? We've already agreed it's none of those things (although they are all helpful). They have very intentionally designed the life they want to live. One that keeps them true to their personal values, living with authenticity, leveraging habits, intentionally growing, living in purpose, and building their personal and professional legacy! It takes time and effort to design a life that allows you to live in freedom. Sometimes it takes a lifetime. This book is designed to provide you with a framework to accelerate the process for you – taking steps forward in each area of your life:

Personal

You will learn we attract what we focus on, why being a workaholic is not a badge of honor, and some guidelines for maintaining balance. Knowing who we are personally and living in our most authentic selves sets us free to gift our best to the world. It's also important to create daily personal habits that fuel our health and overall wellbeing. Although we often have a professional development plan, we neglect to create a personal one for ourselves. We all have thoughts around what we want to "gift" to the world and how we want to be remembered when we're gone, we just don't have a plan for moving us toward it. We'll review tools and resources that can help you build your own framework that can lead you to personal freedom.

Professional

We'll first discuss the importance and components of a professional operating system. Starting by knowing your vision and values, designing an operating system that moves you to the next level, and living out your purpose. You'll identify your priorities and have a framework for keeping the main thing, the main thing. You'll experience how doing all of the above eliminates noise and chaos and brings freedom to your position or organization. When we are leaning into that, we make our organizations and everyone around us better. I also discuss how the 4 components of that can move you from surviving to thriving and explain how you can build your own.

Family

Isn't it interesting that we spend more time planning a vacation than we do planning our family's success? Not because that success isn't important to us. The barriers are twofold: 1. We don't have a framework that supports our family's success. 2. We're struggling to survive daily with too much on our plates. We're overcommitted, overextended, and have very few boundaries to create balance for our families. Many people struggle with this issue we call "balance." It's simply a capacity or math issue. The problem can be solved in a very practical way. We'll discuss the components of an effective family framework and help you build your own.

Spiritual

Do you currently have a framework to facilitate the important work of feeding your soul? This (for me) is the most important piece. If I can get this one right, it seems to feed into every other area of my life. This piece of your framework can include practices such as prayer, meditation, gratitude, yoga, reading, solitude, breathing exercises, martial arts, etc. The possibilities are almost endless in this area. We'll discuss how creating a framework that reminds us daily of what can keep us grounded, authentic, and contributing our unique gifts and abilities to the world at a very high level. I wrap up this chapter, just like the other 3, with some thoughts on how you can build a framework designed to support your unique spiritual journey.

It's a Journey

I think it is important to note that my journey hasn't been perfect. I have learned a lot during my first 50 years on this planet. The only thing I know for sure is I still have a lot to learn! Most of what I know, or what works for me now, is a result of what went wrong, not necessarily what went right. Some of the mistakes I've made along the way, and learned from, were painful for me and for others. As a matter of fact, most of my lessons came from wrong choices and failing.

When we know better, we can do better. The missing link is the right framework. It's what bridges the gap between *knowing* and *doing*. We all know what we should do. We just need the right framework in place to help us make sure we do it.

Along the way, I will provide tools and a framework you can implement to help you navigate your journey. It is my hope that by the time you get through this short, simple book, you will have made some life-changing discoveries and created a framework for yourself, leading to a path of freedom.

As you think about the framework you're currently operating in, I want you to think about the answer to these two questions:

Is the life you're living keeping you from the life you want to live?

How would the right framework set you free to live the life you want to live?

Before we dive into our work in the 4 areas, take 5 minutes to complete this quick assessment. It'll help identify a baseline for where you are in your journey, and where the biggest opportunity lies for you.

You can find the assessment at http://www.michellehubert.com/free-workbook. It is the first part of a workbook designed to help you take steps forward.

Let's take steps to Embrace YOU – Design Your Life – Build your Legacy…creating more freedom into your life!

Part I

———— ∿ ————

JOURNEY TO FREEDOM

Chapter I

PERSONAL FREEDOM

"It's not who you are that holds you
back, it's who you think you're not."
— Denis Waitley

What does freedom mean to you personally?

Is it:

Letting go of limiting beliefs and living
courageously in authenticity?

Breaking free from whatever is holding you back
and living a life of your own design?

Think about what freedom means for you as a person. Outside of any role you may play as an employee, business owner, husband, wife, mother, father, etc. Personal freedom is breaking free from whatever is holding you back. Sometimes we are held captive by our own limiting beliefs or by the stories we tell ourselves. Once we uncover and release our limiting beliefs, grounding our lives in gratitude can help us shape a new story. The story intended for us all along.

It means having a daily routine that helps us operate at our best. Bringing more intention into our lives. Being alive, present, and in alignment with the plan the universe has for us. Remembering every day, the daily choices we make are what shape the life we're living. Those choices are either moving us closer to our purpose or taking us further from it. Personal freedom is not about perfection. It's about designing a framework for living that supports continuous improvement and alignment with purpose. Living with personal freedom means our daily decisions align with our beliefs and personal values, allowing us to make a positive contribution to the world.

Going deeper, personal freedom is about surrendering to who we are and being able to live with full transparency and vulnerability. Many people think those things are a sign of weakness, but the best way to have a positive impact on others is to completely surrender to who we are individually. To be fully transparent at all times. To use our vulnerability to help others realize we're all in this together. Look around you. I'll bet the people you love most in your life are those who are transparent and vulnerable with you, and as a result, you're able to exist comfortably in that space with them. Transparency and vulnerability lead to authenticity.

Freedom is about being bold and courageous enough to be the most authentic version of ourselves. We need to examine what might be keeping us from freedom. It starts with our beliefs. Think about the ones that are determining your current direction. Do they truly belong *to you*, or were they placed *in you* by someone else?

LETTING GO

It is about releasing beliefs that do not align with the person we were meant to be. Letting go of who we aren't and wanting what we don't have. Only then can we move toward loving who we are and recognize and appreciate what we do have.

Write YOUR Story

If you have a vision for your personal life and you aren't living it out it currently, what's stopping you? Many people are too focused on who they believe they aren't to recognize who they truly are.

At some point early in our lives, many of us experience things that throw us off balance. Maybe a parent withholds love, a coach tells us we will never be good enough, or a teacher makes a random hurtful comment. Physical, sexual, or emotional abuse would be extreme examples. It isn't the pain of the event that keeps us from our very best, it's the story we start to tell ourselves about it. As a result, we start to form beliefs about ourselves. We think we will never be good, smart, attractive enough, etc.

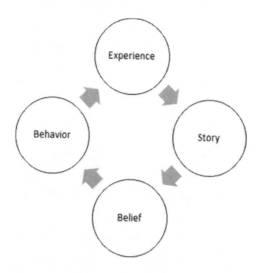

Maybe you can relate to statements such as:

- I'm not smart (or pretty, or interesting, or funny) enough.
- People only value me for what I do, not who I am.
- I'm not talented enough to pursue my passion.
- I need to be perfect to be loved and valued.
- Relationships always end in heartbreak.
- A high level of success is unattainable for me.
- I am not worthy of being loved.
- Only the lucky people succeed at what they care about.

The list could go on and on. At the root, all limiting beliefs tie to stories of either inadequacy or insignificance.

Living within those limiting beliefs can lead to destructive behavior because we're constantly trying to prove our worth. Personal freedom is about the journey of working through those experiences and setting ourselves free from them. It's not the pain of the event that causes all of the negative emotion and decisions, it's how we interpret, react, and respond to the event. It's about refusing to buy into the lies, and instead, buying into the fact that each of us is perfectly designed to serve very important roles in this world.

We all buy into identities that are not our own, we've adopted them in response to some event in our lives. See if any of these sounds familiar to you:

Holly Hiding –Being introverted and shy made it hard for Holly to fit in as a child. She was made fun of relentlessly. Her lack of confidence created a belief that she can't be herself, because other people will judge her.

The fact that she's hiding who she really is keeps her from being authentic. It also keeps her from contributing to the world in the way only she can. Everyone around her gets cheated out of her unique gifts. She's constantly trying to be who others think she should be.

Holly could embrace these beliefs instead:

- *"The only person I need to please is myself – then I can contribute to others."*
- *"I need to be true to me. There'll never be anyone else like me."*
- *"I can't uncover my unique gifts if I'm hiding behind who I think others want me to be."*

Wally Workaholic – Lack of love and affection early in Wally's life caused him to adopt the limiting belief that he is not worthy. He believes he has to do more than anyone else to be successful and gain acceptance. That belief keeps him on a treadmill going faster and faster, trying to prove himself to everyone around him.

He wears workaholism like a badge of honor. His obsession with performance keeps him from healthy relationships in every area of his life.

Wally could embrace these beliefs instead:

- *"I can contribute without holding myself to an unreasonable standard."*
- *"My value comes from who I am, not how I perform."*
- *"My greatest contribution is to myself and my family."*

Polly Perfectionist – Polly learned early in life that perfection was the only standard acceptable in her family. Polly lives, primarily, in a cloud of perceived failure because she believes nothing short of perfection is good enough. She's constantly striving for a standard that can never be met. She judges herself relentlessly and believes her value comes from creating a picture-perfect world. Her pursuit of perfection keeps her from really being present in her life. Everyone around her is impacted because they can't live up to her standards.

Polly could embrace these beliefs instead:

- *"Perfection is not possible, I choose to be present instead."*
- *"My best is always good enough."*
- *"Progress is the standard I need to pursue."*

These are just a few examples of how limiting beliefs can show up in our lives in a way that keeps us from being our best and delivering our best to those around us. Who do you most relate to? Most people find that they are a combination of all three.

There are many more identities we could explore, but you get the idea. If we don't recognize and deal with them, limiting beliefs will show up and hold us back in every corner of our lives. We'll be revisiting Holly, Wally, and Polly as we explore other areas of our lives.

Breaking free is a process. We need to:

1. Recognize the event that led to the belief holding us back.
2. Acknowledge the lie or story we've attached to that event and abandon it.
3. Recognize the judgment we place as a result and extend grace to ourselves and others.
4. Re-establish the truth and ground ourselves in it.

We need to uncover limiting beliefs, understand how they were formed, disrupt the limiting patterns that create them, and begin to write a new story around ourselves and our world.

Anything negative, thoughts were not there when we were born, they are unwelcome guests in our lives that keep us from our very best. It's time to recognize them for what they are, kick them to the curb, and replace them with our true beliefs.

We need to change the message constantly playing in our heads, and the vision we have for our lives.

Ground it With Gratitude

"Gratitude makes sense of our past, brings peace for today, and creates vision for tomorrow."
--- Zig Ziglar

Gratitude is a powerful way to replace the negative dialog that plays in our minds. We can practice gratitude in many ways. From prayer to meditation, to keeping a gratitude journal, to sending handwritten notes, the list could go on and on. The more time of our day we can spend on gratitude, the less time we spend on any negative emotion. Here's the truth: It's impossible to be in anger or fear when we're in gratitude. Just try it. If you're sincerely in gratitude, truly experiencing appreciation for something or someone, it's impossible to stay in anger or fear.

It is also impossible to be in gratitude and in comparison at the same time. If we focus on being grateful for what we have, there is less focus on what we don't have. It's about living from the perspective of wanting what we have, not having what we want.

Adding the practice of gratitude to our lives:

- Makes us happier, friendlier, more social, and more helpful to others.
- Increases our sleep quality and duration.
- Decreases the time it takes us to fall asleep.
- Creates an antidote to stress.
- Makes us more likely to provide support to other people.
- Increases optimism.
- Can improve our immune function.

Try practicing gratitude last thing before you go to sleep and first thing when you wake up in the morning. When you go to bed, commit to acknowledging at least 5 things you are grateful for in the day that has just passed. In the morning, express gratitude for at least 5 things you anticipate during the day. Observe how it changes your perspective throughout the day and begins to change your internal dialog. Side note: Do you have trouble going to sleep or going back to sleep? Reviewing a list in your mind of everything in your life you are grateful for will keep your mind focused on the positive. It also creates a relaxation response. It's a great trick to keep your mind off of your endless to-do list and relax your way into a restful sleep!

The next step is to move from *feeling* gratitude to actually expressing it. Feeling grateful can redirect our lives and our internal dialog in a very positive way. *Expressing* gratitude is like a double bonus. We get all of the benefits of feeling grateful. At the same time, we get the added benefit of having a positive impact on someone else. Look for opportunities to express gratitude to the people in your life. A sincere compliment, a handwritten note, a well-timed text or voicemail, or a small gift of appreciation can change the trajectory of your day and the day of the person you're acknowledging.

Breaking through limiting beliefs and living with gratitude moves us closer to being the authors of our own stories.

Let's move past who you think you're not and discover who you really are!

Living Courageously

Fear is the biggest barrier to living courageously. We have to be undeniably grounded in who we are and become the authors of own story. That is what allows us to be bold and courageous enough to live the life intended for us. It is impossible to completely eliminate fear. But it is possible to create a framework for our lives, which allows us to actively and consistently override it.

Discover What Drives You

Motivational speaker Simon Sinek teaches us to "start with why." His message is primarily focused on knowing why we do what we do in any organization. It applies to our personal lives as well. It is important to know what drives you, what brings you joy, what inspires you, and what you feel your gift to the world is. There are two components in discovering your why. The first one is clarifying your values. The second component is writing a personal mission statement.

If you've never done the work of discovering your values, now is the time! It's important to identify three to five values that truly reflect you. They should create an emotional response in you. They are so true to you, there isn't any way they could be removed from your DNA.

Take a look at the list of words below. As you reflect on the list, ask yourself these questions:

What drives you?
What brings you joy?
What breaks your heart?
What inspires you?
What is your gift to the world?

- Authenticity
- Achievement
- Adventure
- Authority
- Autonomy
- Balance
- Beauty
- Boldness
- Compassion
- Challenge
- Citizenship
- Community
- Competency
- Contribution
- Creativity
- Curiosity
- Determination
- Fairness
- Faith
- Fame
- Friendships
- Fun
- Growth
- Happiness
- Honesty
- Humor
- Influence
- Inner Harmony
- Justice
- Kindness
- Knowledge
- Leadership
- Learning
- Love
- Loyalty
- Meaningful Work
- Openness
- Optimism
- Peace
- Pleasure
- Poise
- Popularity
- Recognition
- Religion
- Reputation
- Respect
- Responsibility
- Security
- Self-Respect
- Service
- Spirituality
- Stability
- Success
- Status
- Trustworthiness
- Wealth
- Wisdom

Circle 10 you feel best describe you.

Now that you've narrowed it to 10, review them again, and eliminate any that are repetitive, or essentially mean the same thing to you.

Take another pass, and try to identify your top 5. Remember, the goal is to get to who YOU really are. Remove ones you "think you should be." The important thing is your values are reflective of you and the way you are wired.

It takes time for most people to truly identify their core values. You might need to live with those 5 for a while to see what really resonates and sticks with you. The longest journey is from your head to your heart, so be patient with yourself in this discovery process. By the end of this book, you will likely be able to come back, and you'll clearly know which 3-5 are really reflective of what's in your heart. Once you do know, your life will never be the same. Once our values are clear, decisions become easy. They become the cornerstones we measure everything against. We get to experience the freedom of living fully in our values, rather than the pain of living outside of them.

Having a personal mission statement empowers you and reminds you why you get up every morning. It is a reminder of your gift to the world and how you want to deliver it. It provides the foundation of your personal framework.

You can start by thinking about what you're good at. Think about the things you are recognized for, seem to come easily for you, and bring you joy.

My personal mission statement is to live a life that is balanced, organized, and structured in a way that allows me to spend the majority of my time helping others. It is true to me because I thrive when I live in a world that is organized. I am at my best when I have a framework or structure to operate within. My passion is being able to make some contribution to others – it's when I'm the most energized and joyful.

You often hear people talk about being "in the zone." I am sure you have had that feeling at some point. Like you are firing on all cylinders, and you are unstoppable. Typically, when people are living out their mission, they report feeling a rush of adrenaline. What generates that for you? What brings you peace and joy? Both components exist in my personal mission. Being balanced, organized, and structured brings me peace. When I'm contributing to others, I often feel I'm operating in my calling, and it energizes me.

Start with your list of potential core values and then put some thought into the answers to the questions we've already reflected on:

What are you passionate about?
What brings you joy/peace?
What would you every day if money weren't in the equation?
What do people most often recognize or thank you for?
What would you like to be remembered for?

Just as we discussed with core values, discovering your personal mission statement is likely a process, not an event. You will need to put some thought into it. You may want to reach out to a few people who know you best and seek their input. It could be something as simple as "I choose simplicity and connection." Just be careful to arrive at a personal mission statement true to you. It can take months to get it identified. I discovered mine 10 years ago. Here's how I know I got it right: It's even truer today than it was for me then.

Every decision I make personally, I weigh against that statement. Discerning if what I'm considering will pull me closer to or take me away from it. That's the power your personal mission statement will hold for you. Your values and mission statement will serve as your compass and guide you to a life designed to fulfill your story.

Live in Authenticity

Authenticity is about having the same fundamental character in different environments. It's about how people experience you. You know people who are very different in their personal and professional lives. It can be confusing to try to figure out who they really are. Are you consistent in word and deed? Do people find you to be predictable in the way they experience you? It's also about being transparent and comfortable with your past. It is acknowledging life hasn't been perfect, but every season has added a different texture to who you are.

Just as with gratitude, one of the greatest gifts of authenticity is it delivers us from comparison. It sets us free to live our life with no filter. It gives us permission to lead the life intended for us, not the Pinterest perfect life we see all over social media. Not that there is anything wrong with getting great ideas that can enhance our lives. There is something wrong, though, with building a life you think is "expected," or living according to someone else's standard. It can be exhausting to constantly try to measure up to who we think the world, or more intimately, those closest to us think we should be. If there are people in your life who don't appreciate you for who you are, they aren't part of your tribe.

"Give up being perfect for being authentic."
---Hal Elrod

Rather than wasting energy striving to be someone or something we're not, we need to invest our energy in helping us live more fully as who we are. Once we clarify our core values and personal mission statement, we can lean into them. They give us permission to be transparent. We get to experience the freedom of fully living our values, rather than the pain of living outside of them. When we can embrace the most authentic version of ourselves, it positions us to deliver what only we can to the world. You never know who needs you – the authentic version of you. There is someone out there you were put on this earth to help, and they need you to be YOU.

Breaking Free

Breaking free is about setting your intention and then building a life around supporting it. It's about leveraging daily decisions or habits that can facilitate you moving from intention into action.

Live with Intention

How do we build intention into our lives? There's been a lot of talk and books written about balance, but let's move beyond balance into intention. Balance is elusive, and there is an ebb and flow to it with each season of our lives. Focusing on intention grounds us in our values and mission and provides the foundation for daily decisions we make.

Consider this for building a framework around intention: There are 168 hours in a week. In your ideal world, how would you like to spend those hours? How many hours a week do you need for sleep? 50? 60? How many hours do you spend each week working? 40? 50? 60? How many hours are left for the 2 major categories left in your life: family and development?

Let's break it down.

Sleep

Determine how many hours per week you need for sleep. What's the magic number that helps you operate at your best?

Work

How many hours do you work per week? Include time at home for your contribution to the family chores. Is it 8 hours per day and then another hour at home for chores?

Family

How many hours per week do you spend with family or close friends? How many would you like to spend if you were being more intentional?

Development

After you've taken care of yourself (sleep), fulfilled your duties at work and at home, spent some quality time with family or friends, what time is left for you to spend with YOU? It's about making time for the things that bring you joy, or in pursuit of personal growth. Exercise, reading, gardening, learning – whatever makes you a better version of yourself is worth exploring.

Allocate your 168 hours however it makes sense for you:

Sleep: 50 hours
Work: 50 hours
Family: 50 hours
Growth: 18 hours

Obviously, there can be crossover in family and growth. You may leverage your commute to and from work for development (audiobooks or podcasts). It's not about actually measuring the hours every day, it's about setting the intention. Having a framework helps us to allocate our effort and energy. Building daily decisions into our lives that are reflective of our values and mission.

Each of us is responsible for our own personal development. True, whether we recognize it or not. Many people do not have a plan for intentional self-development. Why is that? We all know the saying, "If you're not growing, you're dying." It applies to our businesses, professional lives, and to us each personally as well. A very small percentage of the population invests eighteen hours a week in their own growth. We're settling for what life is giving us rather than pursuing the things that bring us joy and make us better. No matter the areas in which we want to improve, imagine a world where everyone invests eighteen hours a week to become the very best version of themselves they can be! For themselves and for their families. That's the kind of world I want to help build for my boys to live in.

We will never be in perfect balance but building a framework can give us a big-picture view. We then evaluate if our intention is matching up with the action we're taking. I think back to when I was working sixty hours a week and twenty more on the weekend. We have to set boundaries and develop a framework for how much time in any category is too much. It is a powerful step toward moving out of chaos and into freedom.

Decide Daily

Show me your calendar, and I'll tell you what's important to you. Do the things in your calendar correlate with your values and mission? Do the daily decisions you're currently making create a framework that supports the life you'd like to live? Let's start at the beginning…

Start STRONG

Many people live in chaos in the morning and don't even realize they are creating it for themselves. They have no intention in their routine. They hit the snooze repeatedly, get ready in a cloud of chaos, fight with the kids, and forget to even acknowledge their spouse on the way out the door.

The book, *Miracle Morning* by Hal Elrod, recommends a framework built around six activities you can do every morning. It is about creating your personal Miracle Morning.

Let's make sure you have a framework that brings peace and freedom into your life. Sets your day up for success and feeds your soul. Here are my key components:

Meditation

Are your mind and body running when they should be resting? Do you avoid silence and stillness? Many people feel as if their mind is constantly racing, and they can't even get a moment of peace. If you have not tried incorporating the practice of meditation into your morning, I highly recommend it. Even 10 minutes can be life-changing. I have found the more I practice meditation, the more often stillness happens when I'm not actively seeking it. Meditation leaves us more grounded and at peace. It helps us stay focused on being present rather than perfect. If you're new to it, I recommend using an app. I use Calm, but there are many out there to guide you.

Exercise

Is your body telling you that your current framework isn't working for you? What are you doing to keep your body moving? I prefer running or walking, but anything constituting movement of some kind falls into this category. There's something about fresh air, a sunrise, and physical activity that makes me feel invincible. Other alternatives are weight lifting, yoga, stretching, spin classes, etc. Just moving can be the fuel we need to get our day started on a positive note. We have to take care of our bodies to be able to contribute to the world. Being physically depleted robs us of our energy and keeps us from delivering our best.

Reading

Five years from now, our lives will be the same except for the people we meet (the relationships we build) and the books we read. A very dear mentor taught me that more than twenty years ago. It's been true for me, and I suspect it's true for you, too. I read books that promote my personal and professional growth as well as a daily devotional. It's important to set the right frame of mind as we go into our day and interact with our families.

If you don't consider yourself a reader, think about the potential impact of this: If you read a chapter a day (for twenty to thirty minutes), and the average book has ten chapters, you'll have read thirty-six more books in the coming year than you read last year. If you're reading the right content, there is no way it won't be life-changing in a very powerful and positive way. Read fiction for pleasure or entertainment, but be sure to pursue growth through reading something that will help you develop in some area of your life. The key is to reserve twenty to thirty minutes a day for intentional growth.

There are many other practices you can consider for your morning routine:

Writing – A gratitude journal or that blog you've been thinking about.

Affirmations – Reinforcing positive thoughts that affirm the person you're becoming.

Listening – There are so many enriching messages out there in podcasts.

Visioning – Create a vision board and spend a moment or two each morning reflecting on it.

Hydrating – Some people swear by drinking water as the very the first part of their routine.

I know on the days I execute my own personal Miracle Morning, I feel bulletproof, as if I can handle any challenge coming my way. Conversely, on the mornings I don't, I feel vulnerable, and small things quickly become larger. Being exhausted and depleted brings out the worst and most vulnerable part of us.

We have very little to give anybody else when we're running on empty. Small annoyances come at us and look like giant setbacks. We're vulnerable when we don't get enough sleep, don't get any physical activity, and don't take good care of ourselves. We need more life-giving practices in our lives.

The law of attraction teaches us it's important we state what we want in positive terms instead of focusing on what we don't want. If we focus on the negativity in our lives, we will attract more negativity into our lives.

This is why gratitude is so important. Being constantly thankful for even the small joys we experience reminds us of the good things happening in our lives. When we focus on the positive, we attract more good things to us.

Deciding daily is about building a framework that provides discipline and habits when there is no motivation. We have to create a world for ourselves where discipline can take over for us in the absence of motivation. It's the path to freedom and to moving into the life we want to live. We can't be a light for others if we don't do things to light our own lamps.

In this chapter, we've discussed letting go, living courageously, and breaking free.

What framework will you design to facilitate and maintain personal freedom? I love the quote below from Wes Swank, who was a well-regarded hedge-fund executive:

"I go to work every day with people who are smarter than me and who are better at what they do. I go to the gym every day and work out with people who are stronger and faster than me. I spend my spare time with friends and family whose values and quality of character I aspire to reflect. For all these reasons, I get a little better, every day."

Wes Swank

It's about getting a little better every day and building a personal framework to support our journey.

Are you holding onto limiting beliefs that are keeping you from living authentically?

What daily decisions to you need to make to build a bridge to the life you want to live?

Embrace YOU – Change your thought process. Move away from fear and limiting beliefs and into gratitude. Discover your values and personal mission and live fully in who YOU are!

Design Your Life – Create a framework that supports the life you want to live. Bring intention to your daily decisions, so they align with and are reflected in your mission and values.

Build Your Legacy – Leverage your values and mission to help you focus on what you are contributing to those closest to you. Start delivering the best version of yourself. Leading to a gift that will be unwrapped long after you are gone.

Our journey to freedom is about progress, not perfection. If you feel "there is a lot to do" to build your ideal personal framework, don't be overwhelmed. Select 1 or 2 practices that will move you in the right direction and start on those today.

Living with authenticity and intention frees us to design the life we want to live. It provides us with the foundation we need to deliver our unique gifts to the world.

When we have a strong personal framework in place, it creates a springboard for success in our professional lives.

Chapter 2

PROFESSIONAL FREEDOM

"Anxiety is caused by a lack of control, organization, preparation, and action."

—David Kekich

What does freedom mean to you professionally?

Is it:

Moving out of chaos and into purpose?
Designing your own professional destiny?

At the beginning of our professional journey, whether we've accepted a new position or we're starting our own business, plenty of fuel is always available to propel us forward. By *fuel*, I mean passion, excitement, drive, determination, and pure adrenaline. We're excited and on a mission to prove that we can be successful in our new endeavor. Meeting our new co-workers for the first time, we are filled with hope and possibility. Anxious to develop relationships and contribute to the greater good in the role that we are in.

It's that enthusiasm that exists at the beginning of any endeavor. Everything is wonderful, and everyone is amazing. We don't notice little annoyances or focus on anything negative. We're so blinded with the possibilities that we don't even notice anything that doesn't align with them.

Then, at some point along the way, real life sets in. Challenges and setbacks creep in. People disappoint us. We disappoint them. We often become distracted by all the obstacles cluttering our path to success. Regardless of our title or position, we are bombarded by all kinds of distractions, emergencies, and competing priorities every day. And then there is the barrage of emails and phone calls constantly requiring our attention. When we don't have a framework for dealing with all the things that come up, they can be overwhelming and frustrating. We get caught up in reacting rather than contributing.

How does all of that reacting show up in our professional lives? You've experienced it out there. When you ask most people how their day is going, often, the answer is "Fine" or "Ok I guess." That's not acceptable. FINE is not acceptable. We deserve so much more than "fine" or "ok." You have experienced people who live in that "victim" mindset. You may have one on your team currently. The world is out to get them, and nothing ever goes their way. They never get the "good projects" or the promotion they've been wanting. They've been *wanting* it, they just haven't been *working* toward it. They are more worried about what they are receiving than what they are contributing. They often want credit when things go well, but never take responsibility when they go wrong. They are so busy operating in a cloud of reactive dust that they never contribute at a level that brings good things their way.

How do we avoid becoming that person? We have to design a life that leads to a different answer. A life that would lead us to say something completely different. Something like "I'm FANTASTIC!" or "I'm so excited about what we're accomplishing!" or "I'm so encouraged by our progress on this project!" or "I love working with this team!" In order to put ourselves in a position for THAT kind of response daily, we need to find ways to:

- Embrace our strengths and leverage them to bring value to our organizations.
- Design a life that facilitates success and helps us execute our personal growth plan.
- Build a legacy that keeps us in purpose and contributing at a high level.

If we were living into *that* each day, we'd feel so much more alive. Our day would be much different. We would spend more of our time being proactive rather than reactive, and our response to "How are you?" would be different, too. We would experience more success and feel more joy. Radiating that out into the world would attract more amazing people to our organizations. It would also facilitate higher levels of success.

When we have a strong professional framework to operate within, we can accomplish the following:

1. Deal with issues, obstacles, and setbacks effectively.
2. Plug everything that comes at us daily into a solid framework.
3. Free up time, effort, and energy to live within our unique abilities.

LETTING GO

Professionally, letting go is about building a framework that keeps us spending the majority of our time on the most important things. Leaving little room for chaos and distractions, creating more freedom. It's about making sure that we create boundaries that allow us to focus on what is really important.

First Things First

In his book, *First Things First*, Stephen Covey shares a story that illustrates how we have to be intentional about allocating our time and how it's critical to prioritize the important things.

A professor takes a pickle jar and begins to fill it with sand, gravel, and water, which represent the small priorities in our lives. Then he tries to add rocks, symbolizing important priorities in our lives, into the jar, but it's already full. The point of this demonstration is that if you allow your jar, or life, to fill up with sand (noise, chaos, distractions—little stuff), then there will be no room for the *big*, important things, or the rocks.

The idea is that you always want to put the big rocks in first—the important things that are foundational to your business or your life. Then you add the small rocks, the things that we need to do but aren't really foundational. Only then do you allow the sand in the small space that remains. At that point, there is very little room for the chaos or distractions, and there seems to be less to deal with.

Here is what Covey says:

> With the "more is better" paradigm, we're always trying to fit more activities into the time we have. But what does it matter how much we do if what we're doing isn't what matters most? . . . If we put other activities—the water, sand, and gravel—in first and then try to fit the big rocks in, not only will they not fit, we'll end up making a pretty big mess in the process. But if

we know what the big rocks are and put them in first, it's amazing how many of them we can put in—and how much of the sand, gravel, and water fits in between the spaces.[1]

Do you put the BIG rocks in first in your professional life? One way to do that is to post a calendar on the wall. When doing annual planning, plug in the most important activities for your role or organization. It can be a powerful visual reminder of what is most important, and it will provide a strong foundation to operate from. Getting the important things in first leaves very little room for noise and chaos to creep in. It also clearly communicates what is important to other team members. It's so easy for items to eat up our time and resources that are not moving us forward.

This concept also applies to our to-do lists. Do you reprioritize every day, moving the big rocks to the top? Or do you do what most people do (it is simply human nature) and cherry pick the items you *want* to do. We tend to "hide" from the things we don't like to do by staying busy with the things that we do like to do. Moving the most

---

[1]. Stephen R. Covey, A. Roger Merrill, and Rebecca R. Merrill, *First Things First* (New York: Fireside, 1994), 89.

important items, or rocks, to the top of your to-do list and tackling those first *every day* will change your life. Remember, it's never something big that makes the biggest impact. It's the accumulation of little things done over time.

"If you take care of the important things,
the urgent things don't show up as often.
The opposite is never true."

—Seth Godin

Putting the bigger "rocks" into our schedule first also helps us assess whether we are spending our time in activities that move us closer to our goals.

Building Boundaries

It's just as important to evaluate what we should stop doing as it is to assess what we should continue doing.

Building appropriate boundaries can help us stay focused on our goals and contributing at a high level.

You've experienced people that have no boundaries. They say yes to everything. Everyone knows they can enlist that person's help. Often, they overcommit, and at the expense of more important items. Stress, anxiety, and burn-out are written all over them. This is an area that I struggle with; I'm a "helper." You can tell from my personal mission statement that I want to help others. That's a good thing as long as it's kept in check. Often, strengths that are unchecked will lead us away from what we're trying to accomplish. Building the appropriate boundaries can help us discern what we should be saying yes to.

Here are some recommendations for building boundaries:

1. Turn off notifications on your phone. Start with email and social media notifications.
2. Turn off notifications on your computer – or close your email when you're not working on it.
3. Block specific times of day for returning calls or emails.
4. Block time into your week for proactive activities – the ones that help you move things forward.

5. Preserve white space in your calendar for you to use as needed.

The thought of turning off notifications on your phone may make you break into a cold sweat, but trust me, it's liberating! We really do not need to know the second that someone posts something. Reading or reacting to it every moment distracts us from delivering our very best. Even turning off your email notifications on your computer can help with focus. That little pop up telling you that you have a new email takes you out of what you're currently working on and disrupts your work, even if momentarily. Unless you have a position that requires it, in most cases, you do not have to return a call or email immediately. Stay focused on what you are doing that is proactive, and use a specific time block to "catch up" on phone calls and emails. Be sure that you're blocking time for accomplishing tasks or driving strategy. And finally, don't forget to leave some white space in your calendar that you can use as needed. Maybe taking a break, checking in to help a partner, or tackling the priority that just came up.

Distraction lowers productivity. Notifications, emails, phone calls, and other interruptions that come at us all day/every day are filled with other people's to-do list and agendas. It's important to serve as a resource and help others, but not at the expense of delivering our very best to those counting on us.

Build some boundaries today that corral the chaos and create more freedom!

LIVING COURAGEOUSLY

Let's be BOLD in designing the life we want to live. That includes bringing the authenticity we discussed in the personal chapter into your organization. It also includes attacking our careers with missionary zeal!

Owning Authenticity

Having our rocks appropriately prioritized and boundaries in place makes room for authenticity. It creates confidence in our gifts, and what we can contribute to our organizations. It removes the fear that we are not good enough.

We spend the majority of our day with the people that we work with. To a large degree, our success is a reflection of the relationships we have with those we work with daily. We need each other to be successful. It's impossible to build deep relationships and create high levels of success if we aren't being authentic.

When we are able to be transparent and authentic, those around us start to feel as if they truly know us. We become predictable and create a safe space for them. What an amazing gift to be able to give the people that you spend most of your daytime hours with.

Deeper connections and daily consistency are keys to success, both personally and professionally. Authenticity is what facilitates deeper connections and frees you to deliver your unique gifts to the world.

Make it a Mission

No matter your profession or position, you can make it a job, you can make it a career, or you can make it a mission. Something changes when you are on a mission every day to serve your organization and customers in a way that only you can.

The reality is that whether we earn a "paycheck" or we operate our own business, we are all "business owners." Whether a CEO or Administrative Assistant, we *own* some part of a business. It's the agreement we make when we accept a position. The terms of the agreement are twofold:

1. Compensation
2. Expectations

In return for whatever compensation we receive, we agree to steward (or own) the part of a business assigned to us. It's incumbent upon us to bring the same level of energy and commitment that we would if we, in fact, owned the business. We're entrusted to create a return on the investment that is being made in us. We should take great pride and ownership in our contribution, whether we literally own the business or not. The path to the next promotion is to become a ROCKSTAR in the position that we are currently in. Taking tremendous pride in our results and the way we get them. Striving to bring value to everyone around us. Not striving to make ourselves look good, but to make everyone around us look good. Let's be on a mission every day to serve our organizations and customers in a way that only we can.

Making it a mission means dressing for and conducting ourselves for the position that is two levels above us. If you want to be a CEO someday, start dressing like one. Start carrying yourself with that level of professionalism. Start contributing at that level. Make it your mission to become a master of execution.

Making it a mission requires that you have a vision that ignites passion.

BREAKING FREE

The final piece, professionally, is breaking free from all of the chaos and building a framework that brings peace and consistency to you and to others around you. That includes developing a growth plan that keeps us inspired and contributing to our organizations at a very high level

From Surviving to Thriving

The shift from surviving to thriving happens when we become intentional about 4 areas of our professional lives. There's nothing new in these areas, we've been discussing them. The next step is a shift toward designing the professional life that you want to lead. Taking control and making your current position fit into your utopia.

The 4 areas are:

1. Vision
2. Culture
3. Planning
4. Process

The first two areas focus on *why* we do what we do, and the last two focus on *how*.

Vision – Identifying our vision puts us in a position to choose purpose over popularity. It helps us stay focused on what we believe and what we're striving for. As we discussed before, if you don't have (or haven't been provided with) an organizational vision – create one of your own. It should be more of a discovery process than a creation process. It's already *in* you, you just have to spend some time discovering what drives you. As we discussed earlier in this chapter, once you have your vision identified, establish your values and create value statements.

Think about your "why." As we discussed earlier, author Simon Sinek teaches us that people are attracted to us (or to our business) not based on what we do, but why we do it. You have to be clear on your "why" before you can convey it to others.

Once you start living your vision and values, distractions become easily recognizable. Your vision becomes a filter for decision making.

Your value statements provide a framework for how people experience you. Ideally, it becomes a consistent experience for them. People know what to expect from you.

Culture – Establishing a culture that reflects who we are, and what we stand for allow us to choose surrender over control. When our values consistently show up in our behavior, a culture starts to develop. We can surrender to the culture that we're building rather than trying to micro-manage every detail of our organization.

Simon Sinek puts it this way: Culture = Values X Behavior

You've seen charts that show the difference between managing and leading. Often listed under management are a bunch of task-oriented items. Under leading, there are a lot of items that require influence. We earn the right to influence others by sharing our values and then modeling them consistently. It builds trust and predictability – two key factors that will lead others to follow.

Take a look at your surroundings (your office, cubicle, desk, etc.). What is the story it creates about you or your business? Measure what is going on visually against what is going on internally. Does your space reflect chaos or freedom? We each have control over our environment to an extent. It might be time for you to redesign your space in a way that contributes to the culture you're trying to build. Your surroundings are telling a story about you. You need to be the author of that story.

We are all creating a culture. It's either by design or by default. Often, default cultures are negative and unproductive. A victim mindset prevails. Creating a culture by design for a team of one or one thousand allows you to shape your environment, and the kind of people you want to attract to it. If you want to work with positive people, it starts by building a positive culture to attract them to.

We can't attract the best people to work with us or for us if we don't create a culture that they want to be a part of. People will choose a great culture over income requirements or a great benefit package more often than you think.

When your culture is strong, you can overcome any challenge, setback, or obstacle that comes your way.

Planning – Having a strong planning process professionally allows us to choose the pain of discipline over the pain of regret. It's the piece of our framework that helps us identify the goals we want to accomplish and create a plan to make it happen.

In the absence of a plan, we stumble about day in and day out. We spend all of our time reacting to what's coming at us. We can't figure out how we could possibly have time to accomplish our goals. We drown in emails, return phone calls, and meetings that don't move us closer to where we want to be. We're stressed out, wrung out, and checked out most of the time.

The antidote to all of that is having a plan and then following through with unmatched execution. Execution is the key to success, but before you can execute, you have to know where you're going.

Based on H.L. Hunt's key to success requirements, you can follow a 3-step planning process:

1. **Decide what you want.** Determine the 3-5 most important goals for you professionally at this moment. Make sure they are the 3-5 most important by asking yourself this question: "Would my supervisor agree that these are the goals I should be working toward this year?" or for a business owner, "Would a board of directors agree that these are the 3-5 most important goals for your business." Less is more. In deciding what you want – focus on the few that matter.

2. **Determine the price you'll have to pay to get it.** What would have to happen daily or weekly for you to hit your goals? Think about the resources you would need. You might need to collaborate with others. You'll want to determine the time commitment it would take. Identify the steps you would need to take to hit each goal.

3. **Commit to paying the price.** Make the investment. Block the time. Consult with others who have been successful in that particular area. Outline the steps you'll need to take. Schedule collaboration opportunities in your calendar. Remember, show me your calendar, and

I'll tell you what's important to you. Committing to paying the price means your goals show up in your everyday decisions. Get it down on paper, and make sure you have the steps to achieving your goals built into your schedule. When you prioritize the most important things first, it quiets the chaos around you and creates more freedom.

Process – Having strong processes to lean on creates the opportunity to stay focused on the important rather than the immediate. It allows us to create capacity in our professional lives and provides for innovation.

This is where execution comes in. Having a process daily, weekly, monthly, and annually for how you move things forward. For how you get the most important things done. Is there daily intention for execution that moves you closer to your goals?

Think of the example of writing a book. The goal is to finish it and get it published. Writing the goal down will make it more *likely* to happen but won't make it happen. What will bring the goal to fruition is the daily practice of writing. Execution is all about creating a framework that facilitates the right daily decisions. Goals can be bright, shiny objects and fun to focus on. But it is the little, seemingly monotonous, daily tasks done consistently over time that gets goals accomplished. Execution is a daily grind, it is not glamorous.

In the absence of defined processes, we live in chaos, constantly reinventing the wheel. Chaos breeds anxiety, and they both come when we spend most of our time reacting to emergencies. Many times, the *urgent* shows up masquerading as something *important*. If we don't have a strong framework, we get sucked into the urgent, and it robs us of precious time for the important. The work that moves us closer to our goals and dreams.

In our professional lives, we all have about 5 – 7 core processes that we do over and over again. Those few processes create 80% of our results.

Here's an example of our onboarding process:

Day 1:	**Welcome**
	-Office Orientation
	-Welcome gifts (office supplies, decor and company swag)
	-Team Introduction
Prior to Day 7:	**Formal Orientation**
	-Organizational Overview
	-Job Description and Responsibilities
	-Professional Growth Opportunities

It's an intentional process that has two goals:

1. Cause our new team member to feel welcome and supported.
2. Start the culture-building process, integrating them into our team.

The welcome occurs the first hour of the first day. It creates a framework for making sure we create a positive initial experience. The goal is twofold:

- Create excitement about their new opportunity or position.

- Reassure them that they've made the right decision.

The formal orientation occurs sometime within their first week. The intent of this orientation is to bring them into our organizational story. It affirms that we are who we said we were in the interview process. Our entire team participates in this two-hour meeting, and everyone contributes to the conversation, which initiates the culture-building process.

- The organizational overview casts a vision.
- Reviewing the job description and responsibilities paints a picture of where they fit into the overall vision/organization.
- Sharing how we prioritize and approach professional growth initiates them into our culture. It also reassures them that there is a career path for them within our organization.

That is just one example of a core process. As discussed earlier, most organizations have 5-7 that produce the majority of their results.

How would your professional life change if you:

- Identified those 5 – 7
- Documented the process that works best to achieve each of them
- Repeated those processes over and over – doing it the same way every time
- Created a sustainable, predictable result

We get better by doing something repeatedly. It creates capacity and provides for innovation. Once we document and refine a process, it makes it very easy to teach it to others. Being considered an expert in our field positions us for great opportunities. You become known for what you know. It also creates confidence and peace internally, leading to more freedom!

Vision and culture are about discovering and pursuing our "why." They help us reflect our beliefs and attract people who believe what we believe. Planning and process are about the "how." Building intention into our daily decisions and taking execution to the next level. When we are working in our "why," we are leading ourselves and, often, others. When we're operating in "how," we're executing systems and processes. Freedom comes when those 2 components are so intertwined, it's hard to tell where one ends, and another begins. When our "why" is so strong that it's reflected in everything we do and everything we produce.

Ground it in a Growth Plan

When we find ourselves off track, will we have a foundation to lean on, to *rely* on, to carry us through the journey until our passion and excitement resurface?

Investing in our own professional development can help build and maintain that foundation.

I started investing in professional development early in my career, and it has added tremendous value to every area of my life. I've been in coaching of some form for over 10 years, and I invested in other resources long before that. I need someone to push me, challenge me, and help me create continual growth. If we are not growing, we are dying. That might seem dramatic, but the reality is if we are not moving forward, we are sliding backward. When I plan my year, I consider professional development opportunities for myself and for my team as one of the highest priorities. That is one of the big "rocks" that goes into our calendar first. We're always looking for the next growth opportunity.

Isn't it interesting that you can talk to two different people that attend the same meeting and get very different feedback? One will say that it's the best meeting they've ever attended, and that they have a ton of great takeaways to implement. The next will say that it was the most boring meeting they've ever been to, and it was a total waste of their time. What's the difference? It's the perspective of each person, and what they expected to get from the meeting. It's easy to miss the golden nugget if you're not looking for it!

"People are anxious to improve their circumstances, but they are unwilling to improve themselves; they therefore remain bound."

James Allen

Pastor and leadership author John Maxwell has a process for implementing ideas from any event or meeting he attends. He goes through his notes and categorizes them as follows:

A = Apply to my life
C = Change in my life
T = Transfer or teach to those in my life

He then prioritizes his takeaways, so he can start to implement the items he wants to move forward on. Now that reflects commitment and intention about learning and growing every day. If it's good enough for John Maxwell, it's certainly good enough for me!

You might be familiar with the seventy-two-hour rule. If you do not execute the strategies you learn within seventy-two hours of returning from the event, you are not likely to do so. They will be gone forever. To help ensure that I get the most out of every conference, I block off time on my calendar when I return. I devote that time to identifying which strategies I will implement.

I have learned and grown so much from working with mentors and by investing in paid coaching. If you want to grow beyond your current capacity, consult with someone who will be candid with you. Someone who believes in you and who will push you outside of your comfort zone. Someone who sees more potential in you than you see in yourself. You need feedback and encouragement in your life, and you need to provide it for someone else.

Consider these elements for your Professional Growth Plan:

- Time blocked for daily reading or studying
- Working on a designation or some kind of education/training
- Attending workshops/events that interest you professionally
- Looking for development opportunities outside of your business/industry (Attending Global Leadership Summit for one example)
- Asking someone to mentor you
- Investing in professional coaching

Making the investment in ourselves will provide the framework we need to feed our souls professionally. It provides the springboard that will reignite our passion and give us new energy to move forward. We can't discover new ideas and succeed beyond our wildest dreams if we aren't consistently learning and growing.

Intentional growth helps us stay relevant to our organizations and the industries we serve.

It's about continuous re-invigoration, so that we can accomplish more for our organizations and our families – delivering the very best version of ourselves.

You are in control of your own professional development and destiny…

Remember, show me your calendar, and I'll tell you what your priorities are. How is your growth plan showing up in your calendar?

Too often, we allow ourselves to be victims of our environment or circumstances. This chapter is about taking control professionally and designing a life that leads us to greater levels of success.

Remember **Holly Hiding**? A great framework for her to move forward professionally might include being more confident in sharing ideas rather than holding back. That would allow her to gift more of her talents and abilities to her organization and to build stronger professional connections. **Wally Workaholic** could take a step forward by building some professional boundaries that support balance in his life. Identifying a few hours of the day that are reserved specifically for family could be just the framework he needs. And finally, **Polly Perfectionist** could benefit from a professional growth plan that recognizes her strengths and helps her develop in areas that she may be struggling in. Staying focused on progress – not perfection!

What is missing from your professional framework that would lead you closer to your goals?

Have you taken control of your professional development and your own level of success?

 Embrace YOU – Discover or reconnect with your professional vision and values. Be on a mission to serve your organization and those who benefit from it. Leverage your authenticity to bring what only you can.

 Design Your Life – Create a plan and processes that reflect your goals and dreams. Utilize your calendar to make sure you keep the main thing the main thing. Commit to unmatched execution standards.

 Build Your Legacy – Discover the contribution that only you can make to your organization. Stay focused on what you are contributing, not what you are receiving. Look for ways to mentor and develop others.

Evaluate where you are strong professionally and choose one area that you can take a step forward in today.

Design a professional life that is purpose driven. One that has you on a mission every day – contributing in your own unique way.

Doing the work to deliver the best version of ourselves personally and professionally, creates the freedom to contribute to our families at a higher level.

Chapter 3

FREEDOM FOR YOUR FAMILY

―――――~―――――

"Family is not an important thing; it's everything."

—Michael J Fox

What would freedom look like for your family?

Would it be:

Letting go of the pursuit of perfection and focusing on being present?

Building deeper connections and a framework that leads to less chaos and more freedom?

If family is, in fact, *everything*, as the quote says, how can we bring more intention to making sure we treat it with that kind of reverence?

On the day we get engaged, we're filled with love and hope for the future. We focus on shared beliefs rather than differences and overlook annoying habits. We create a story about our future and the relationship we're entering into. We have a vision for our marriage and are convinced that we'll be together forever.

Flash forward a few years, and things are not so rosy. What happened?

Real life sets in. There are bills to be paid and chores to do. Trash to be taken out and laundry to be done. There are disappointments, hardships, and setbacks. There are growing expenses and empty bank accounts. As our families grow, there are 3am feedings and 3-year-old tantrums. Date nights become few and far between. School activities and homework dominate our lives. Not to mention the constant judgment and comparison. We feel a need to be

Pinterest perfect parents and are rarely fully present. We are constantly running on empty.

No one wakes up one day and says, "I'm going to destroy my family today." It is the little daily decisions made over time that either deepen relationships or damage them. Often, the damage is inadvertent, but that does not make it any less lethal.

What happens when we don't have a framework for navigating challenges? We ignore them. They get worse. Something small grows into something big. And all of a sudden, the issue seems insurmountable. If we were to invest more time, effort, and energy into our family structure, we wouldn't wind up in crises nearly as often. We would solve issues before they got that big. We would invest in our relationships, and we would make sure everybody around us was nurtured, loved, and supported.

People who get married generally love each other, so why is the divorce rate in the United States 40-50%? No one sets out to fail, or even believes it's possible on the day they get married. Many couples lose their way because they don't have a framework to lean on. They don't know what they're trying to accomplish together as a family. They're not investing any time, effort, or energy in the success of their family. When issues arise, they don't have a framework for solving them. They are barely surviving when they could be thriving.

What if we had a framework for our family that helped us be more present, let go of the pursuit of perfection, and build deeper connections?

Let's create a framework for leading well, and loving well, on the home front.

LETTING GO

Letting go is about choosing to be fully present in our families. Letting go of the pursuit of perfection. It's about building boundaries that reduce chaos and bring freedom. It calls us to "build our tribe" with relationships that thrive and enrich our lives.

Present over Perfect

Happiness is found not in having what you want but wanting what you have. Being present over perfect is about being fully present in our lives. It's about feeling and expressing gratitude for what we have. *Wanting what you have* is about fully appreciating the everyday joys that life presents us. That's easy to say and hard to do. Most of the time, we are either reliving something from our past or dreaming (or more likely worrying) about something in the future. We are rarely present "in the moment."

"Most people aren't out of balance, they are into distraction."

—Brendon Burchard

Why are we so addicted to distraction? What are we trying to avoid? Think about the last time you were truly present – for an extended period of time. When you weren't planning, working, pushing, worrying, positioning, pursuing, or any other thing. For most of us, every hour of every day, our minds are wrapped up in something we should have done, or something that we need to be doing.

Can you think of the last time that you were truly present with your family? No distractions. No phone in your hand. *Fully* present with them. Soaking in the moment, fully immersed in the experience of being with them? Not thinking about how things should be, but just finding joy in the way they are?

Somewhere along the way, life got crazy, and most of us bought into it. We somehow started believing that more is better. Striving for some idea of perfection, that when examined closer, is really insanity. This is an area I've struggled with. I am now fiercely committed to getting better. To being more present.

Life is so fragile. I'm recognizing that more and more every day. From my journey with a sister that has survived breast and tongue cancer to losing my "perfectly healthy" mom at 71 to stage 4 lung cancer and an avalanche of health issues that occurred over a 40-day period. And then this morning, a call with a colleague who has already lost one son in a car accident to learn that his 21-year-old son was in an accident last night, and his life is hanging in the balance. It is all around us. There are reminders everywhere of how fragile life can be. My biggest fear these days is that I'm missing it. The clock is ticking, and I may be missing the little moments that mean the most.

My quest is to be more present and to quit worrying about being perfect. There's nothing like a good crisis to rock your world enough to make you hit the reset button. Life has been whispering to me for years to be more present. The last 3 years, that whisper has become a roar, but one that I welcome. I'm paying more attention to the reminders. I am doing something about it. I am building a life that keeps me more present and nudges out the thought of "perfect."

Family Boundaries

> "Learn to say 'no' to the good so you can say 'yes' to the best."
> —John C. Maxwell

Several years ago, I was in a director position at my company. I was partnering with our regional vice president to lead a sales organization of 250 producers who had 500 additional team members. We had 10 sales managers, and I was in charge of their leadership development. It was a position that I loved, serving people that I love in a company that I love. My career was on an intentional path for advancement. There were even a couple of opportunities to pursue a VP position in other states, but the timing wasn't right for us to move. During my 6 years in that role, I traveled the entire state. I loved every minute of it and was successful in serving my organization and my family, all while, traveling a ton of miles. (That could never have happened without the support of a tremendous partner, more to come on that piece later.)

I had built some pretty good boundaries for the time I wasn't traveling. For that season of my life, I cut out everything that didn't include spending time with or supporting my boys. I dropped out of community volunteer positions and social clubs. If I was at home, I wanted to make sure I was with my family. I made nearly every sporting event, even if it meant my day started at 4:00am or ended after midnight. Even though we were able to make that work, and survived that season, I started to realize that we were not thriving.

In the thick of it, when my boys were a junior and senior in high school, an opportunity to greatly reduce my travel and stay closer to home came up. It would be considered a "step back" professionally. I consulted my husband and some trusted mentors. A senior leader in our organization advised me, "You have to decide what you want." The implication was that if I wanted to stay on the executive leadership path that I was on, I needed to stay in the position that I was in. He was an amazing leader, and meant well, but that was incredibly disheartening to me. Could that possibly be true? If I made the best decision for my family, would it derail everything I had worked so hard for? Would it remove me from the "promotion pool?"

After a lot of prayer, I knew exactly what I needed to do. It was crystal clear that I had to choose my family. I also came to the realization that whatever my destiny is will only be positively impacted by the hard choice, which by the way, was 110% the right choice. As the quote above says, I had to say no to something good, so I could say yes to the best – my family.

Fortunately for me, that still meant being in a position that I loved, serving people that I love in a company that I love. Recently, I was promoted into the role I had previously been working toward. Validation that when we make the right decision for the right reasons, it ultimately leads us right where we are supposed to be.

That's just one example of utilizing boundaries to protect our families. We have to stop worrying about what the world needs from us and start paying attention to what our families need from us.

We have to stop the insanity of participating in every sport, club, event, opportunity that is available. We have to stop committing every hour of every day. We have to make space for our families to thrive. We have to start saying *no* more than we say *yes*. Every time we say yes to something, we are saying no to something else. We have to make sure we are saying yes to our families!

"Whenever we say "yes" to something, there is less of us for something else. Let's make sure our "yes" is worth the less."

—Lysa TerKeurst

As you are making decisions that impact your most prized possession, your time with your family, consider these questions:

1. What is my motive for saying yes?
2. Who would it please for me to say yes?
3. What is the cost (time, effort, energy, money) of me saying yes?

4. How will our family be impacted by this yes?

5. How will our family be enriched by this yes?

And here's another tip: Never commit on the spot when it impacts your family. If the ask requires an immediate answer, always make your immediate answer no. Give yourself some time for thoughtful consideration. Be quick to say no and slow to say yes.

LIVING COURAGEOUSLY

Love that Lasts

Are you putting your most important relationship first? This is something that I struggled with for years. We tend to prioritize our careers and our kids above our marriages. That's a recipe for disaster and is reflected in the current divorce rate.

We have to reprioritize the contribution we are making to the world so that we are contributing to our marriages first. Investing in that relationship actually improves every other relationship. Too often, we build a life around our children and their perceived needs. We base our decisions on what they want or what we convince ourselves that they need. Of course, we want to nurture them and help them to develop into amazing little human beings. But putting them first at the expense of our marriages will destroy our marriages and create young adults that think the world should revolve around them. There is no better gift we can give our children than the picture of a marriage and love that lasts. Not one that is perfect, but one that is positive and rewarding.

Here are some behaviors that create barriers to love that lasts:

Scorekeeping - Creating a debt/debtor relationship – you owe me.

Expecting - I'm not going to thank you when you do, but I'm going to ask you when you don't.

Winning – Being more interested in being right than moving forward.

Conforming – Giving up and giving in, building resentment.

You know what each of those looks like. You have either lived it in your own relationships, or you have observed it in others. All of these behaviors lead to leaving. Leaving the relationship mentally and emotionally, even if we haven't left physically.

These behaviors will creep into every relationship from time to time, its human nature. The key to success is recognizing them and redirecting your thoughts (and your heart). Reminding yourself that you are more interested in protecting and deepening the relationship than whatever negative emotion you may be feeling at a given moment.

I am grateful that during the years I traveled a lot, our marriage was strong enough to withstand the challenges we faced. There are a handful of components that made that possible.

5 Key Components to Love that Lasts:

- Love
- Trust
- Respect
- Collaboration
- Grace

The first is love. That's where it all starts. But I am not just referring to falling in love, I'm talking about love as a verb. Love that shows up in our daily actions. It's everyday acts of kindness. It is putting your partner first, racing to the back of the line.

With a foundation of love, you can start to build trust. Building trust takes time. It's the result of delivering on your promises daily. Consistency, day in and day out. It's the reassurance that you are who you say you are, and you will do what you say you will do. You can't be fully intimate with someone you don't give yourself fully to, and you can't give yourself fully to someone you don't trust.

When you love and trust someone, respect starts to grow. You may not always agree, but you can respect each other's viewpoints. You accept each other's strengths and shortcomings. You recognize and acknowledge each other's gifts and achievements. Respect grows from what the other is contributing to your relationship and family.

With love, trust, and respect in place, collaboration can flourish. That is true professionally, and it is just as true personally. Life is so much more fun when we let go of control and lean into collaboration with our partner. I am more worried about *us* winning that

I am about *me* winning. Collaboration can unite us and help us achieve a common vision.

The final piece is grace. It may actually be the most vital. Often, we make the mistake of expecting our partner to "complete" us. We expect them to make all of our dreams come true. That is a ridiculous expectation, and one that is unfair. In embracing ourselves, and in embracing our partners, we need to extend grace. It is allowing for the fact that none of us are perfect. That we will disappoint ourselves and each other from time to time. We are all human. It is the recognition that we are in this together, for the long haul, even when it gets messy. Grace is going to be required to build a love that lasts.

Building love that lasts is the most challenging and the most rewarding endeavor that we'll ever experience. In this season, I am grateful that we have put in the hard work and are now enjoying the fruits of our labor. I am proud of us and the life we have built. It wasn't easy. At times, it was messy. But it was so worth it.

Collaboration over Control

Part of building a love that lasts includes compromise and collaboration. If I am honest, this was likely the most challenging area for us as a couple. We had differing opinions on how to handle issues with the boys, and often, we had to find a way forward that we could both live with. There was no doubt that we both loved them and wanted the best for them. Sometimes (often times really) how we believed that was best achieved was different. Those differences created tension that we had to learn to manage with each other. Maybe you can relate?

When I think of family collaboration, I think of it from 2 perspectives:

- How we collaborate as a couple to operate a successful household.
- How we interact with each other as a family.

We seem to have more stress and less peace as families. Letting go of control and committing to collaboration can help us move in another direction. One that unites us. One that creates more freedom.

Is your household a dictatorship or a democracy?

Think of that question from 2 perspectives:

1. Does every household member contribute to the greater good?
2. Are decisions made individually or collectively?

Daily life seems to go so much better when we are all working together toward the same goals. When everyone feels like they are winning, and no one is losing.

In building a framework for collaboration, assessing capacity is an important component.

The quality-time framework that we operated within served us well and got us through some years when there was a lot of pressure on our schedules and frequent travel. Even so, if I were able to go back, there is definitely one component that I would have fortified for our family. I have uncovered the root cause of the balance issue that is present in so many families. Capacity is at the root of the issue.

When we're operating a business and we have a capacity issue, we either eliminate some of the work being done, or we hire an additional person to solve the capacity issue and move the business forward. For some reason, we don't see it from that same perspective in our families. Whether you are a one-parent or two-parent family, consider implementing the framework I shared in the previous chapter to maximize your 168 hours:

- 50 hours of sleep
- 50 hours in your career/business
- 50 hours with your family
- 18 hours of personal/professional development

Take those 50 hours of family time, and list everything that takes time in your family in a typical week: cooking, cleaning, laundry, homework, eating meals, doing chores, paying bills, lawn care, car maintenance, school/sporting events, dancing, carpool time, game time, church, youth group, etc. (If there are two of you, then you have 100 hours total.)

1. List *everything* you do or that needs to happen in a typical week.
2. Identify the appropriate time it takes to complete each task, activity, or event.

3. Determine which family member to attach that task, activity, or event to.

Now take a look at the time assigned to each family member and how that fits into their individual 50 hours of family time. Is there a balance between Mom and Dad, and are age-appropriate activities assigned to each kid? Is there more to do than the number of hours allotted? Is there any downtime left at all? Is there space for restoration?

If you discover through this process that you have a capacity issue—that you don't have enough time to comfortably accomplish everything on the list—You can solve it 2 ways:

1. Prune some "commitments" out of your life – and your family's life that are not serving you.
2. Hire appropriate help. I hired help with housecleaning and a few other tasks. But looking back now, I wish I had outsourced much more so that I could reclaim those precious hours of quality family time.

If you do not have the funds to hire outside help, asking for age-appropriate help from each child can help solve the capacity issue. This also creates teamwork and ownership within your family framework.

Remember, this is about intention, not necessarily the exact number of hours in a day. Frankly, there are seasons when we spend more or less time in particular areas. That is ok, as long as it is by design. An intentional choice that fits the season you are in. A recipe for disaster is for both parents to be operating completely over capacity for an extended period of time. Resentment and blame start to creep in, which results in a high level of stress and pressure and doesn't allow us to gift our unique abilities to our families. Instead, we're merely trying to survive.

Largely gone are the days of one parent working and one parent doing everything it takes to successfully operate a home. We never replaced that one full-time parent at home. We're just trying to cram everything in that we used to accomplish with one person solely focused on running a successful household (which is not that different from running a successful business).

Collaboration also relates to how we interact with each other within our family. We need to stop trying to control and collaborate more. Stay with me a minute here, I know that is not going to sit well with some of you. I know that, as parents, our job is to keep our kids safe and to nurture them into decent human beings. I have also learned, though, that no matter how much we try to control other people (even our children), we will never be successful. Not long-term anyway. We might "win the moment," but I have realized that even those moments are not wins. When we try to control, all we do is add more tension to the relationship and teach them that love = control.

Think of it from this perspective: A child in the grocery store is throwing a tantrum. As parents, we often have an emotional reaction. We try to control the situation, we try to control the child, who, at that moment, is obviously out of control. We try to control them because we are embarrassed by their behavior. The only thing we can really control is our own response to their behavior. They are children struggling to learn and grow. They are going to be a disaster at times as they learn to deal with their own emotions. We have it backward. We should only be embarrassed if *our* behavior warrants it (and let's be honest, sometimes it does).

The same is true for our teenagers and adult children as well. The more we can compromise and collaborate and move away from control, the less chaos. Yes, it is our job to keep them safe and help them make good decisions. It is their job to push boundaries and grow. Often, there is a middle ground that you can both live with. You can find that middle ground by doing more asking than telling. An added bonus of that approach will be deeper connections. I figured that out as my boys got into high school, but I wish I had much sooner. I think it would have saved us all some battles that did not need to be fought.

This is one reason that we are often better grandparents than parents. Watch grandparents with the little people in their lives. It's a much more collaborative relationship. Of course, the fact that we are older, wiser, and more patient helps as well.

Our job is to love them. Not to judge them, and not to change them. To love them, that's it. Of course, loving them means that there are consequences to wrong behavior and guiding them to good decisions. But from a place of collaboration, not control. At the end of the day, we will not be judged by what others do, but by *our* response. Our response should always be in love.

Take some time today to evaluate if you have a capacity issue and how you'll solve it, so every family member has balance and is contributing their very best to your family. Does a shift need to occur for how you problem-solve as a family? Choose collaboration over control.

BREAKING FREE

How We Do it Here

We know professionally that if you're not running your business, it is running you. In the same way, if you are not running your life, it's running you. The way we take control and move toward the life we want to live is very similar to building a professional framework.

It starts in the same way. With a few nuisances, it mirrors how we successfully build a framework professionally. Defining who we are and what we stand for, investing in people, making good financial decisions, fighting fair, creating traditions, and keeping the main thing, the main thing (putting the rocks in first).

Let's look at these six components of a framework as they apply to our family lives.

1. **Vision**. We hear a lot about the importance of establishing a vision for your business. It's a necessary roadmap for your personal life, too. Your vision for your family is your view of who you are, what you stand for, and what you're trying to accomplish. Establishing your vision and values bring clarity, focus, and fuel to your life. What is your family's gift to the world? What are your family's short and long-term goals? Reference the values list in the Personal Chapter to help you identify your family values.

2. **People**. How can each family member contribute to the overall benefit of the family using their unique talents and abilities? How do the family members interact with each other? Where could each family member be better and do better, and how can you support that?

3. **Finances**. This relates to your budget and net worth. How do you decide what to spend money on? Do you make emotional, financial decisions or do you operate from a budget? Are you making decisions based on your long-term goals or on short-term desires? Regardless of

your net worth today, are you making progress? Are you working toward retirement goals together or just hoping that everything will work out when you get there?

4. **Fighting Fair**. How does your family deal with issues? Do you acknowledge them and set out to resolve them in a healthy, productive way, or do you let them linger? Do you have a process, system or framework for resolving them? In the absence of a framework to operate within and to solve issues, we often assume that any problems we're experiencing are people problems. That's not true 99 percent of the time, we just need a process for solving issues as they arise. Are you collaborating to find solutions together that serve the greater good?

5. **Traditions**. How do you spend your downtime? Do you take a vacation together every year? Do you attend church together on Sundays? Does your family have a date night or intentional time with each individual family member? What about a family game night? These are the things you do on a regular basis

that support being who you are (your vision).

6. **The Main Thing**. Are you identifying your "rocks," or big priorities, tending to them, and continuing to move forward? The best way to do that is to regularly conduct family meetings. Set aside time for Mom and Dad to be intentional about planning for the family. This typically occurs on the deck over a drink for us these days. It provides a great touchpoint for us to check in on our goals and if we are working toward the right priorities. Back to that calendar question again: Are your family's priorities showing up in your calendar? Are you getting the rocks in first?

We have established our vision and values as a family:

Our four core values are: fun, loyalty, teamwork, and service.

Our mission statement is:
As a family, we are at our best when we are serving others.
We will find more time for each other and to entertain others.

We will donate our time, talent, and treasure.
We will be viewed as a family that is fun, loving, committed, and connected.
We will fill our home with laughter.

Our hope is that by being intentional about living out our core values and mission, we can be our best and bring out the best in one another.

We have financial goals that we are working together to reach. We share challenges, concerns, and frustrations, but do not do it with raised voices. We have unspoken rules for fighting fair – we rarely "fight," but if we do, we never disrespect each other or let emotions rule. We know what traditions are important to each other, and we try to build more that keep us connected to our boys. And finally, we evaluate our rocks regularly to make sure we are a united front working toward common goals.

When our two boys, Cayle and Braydon, were growing up, I had not yet discovered the power of living within a framework. But I did some things somewhat accidentally that created a framework for us.

For example, when they were little, my husband liked to golf on men's night, which was every Thursday night. So that became the night when the boys and I would go out to dinner. That became our routine, and a tradition, and we got to spend some quality time together.

Tim and I had regular had date nights. Sometimes by ourselves, and sometimes with other couples. We made time for adult interaction and conversation. We made it a priority to connect with each other. I honestly think if we had not made that commitment and utilized babysitters, we might have gone months at a time without truly connecting. It created opportunities to live and laugh together. Not that we couldn't do those things as a family as well, but it was important to have time and experiences that were just for us.

Instead of taking the two boys school shopping together, I started taking them shopping separately for a weekend. That allowed me to devote my attention to each of my two sons. The trip was about them and what they wanted to do, and we worked-in all their favorites. Now that they are adults, I actually miss those trips, a time for that one-on-one connection. Those traditions were borne out of what our family needed at the time. They became some of our most cherished memories.

I started making it a priority to spend *quality* time with my children because I didn't have the *quantity* of time other parents had. I tried to find opportunities to be more intentional about spending time with them. It wasn't perfect—in fact, those years when I traveled were tough for us.

During that time, a lot of extra responsibility fell on my husband's shoulders. We were able to navigate that season because we had a strong framework and a pretty strong marriage. In any marriage, there are times when you're both under a ton of pressure and stress. But even during that time, neither one of us ever attacked each other or said things to each other that we couldn't take back. His sources of stress were different than mine, but the pressure was equally heavy on both sides. We have a lot of trust and respect for each other, and we are strongly committed to avoiding emotional reactions. We do not let pressure or emotion rule the moment, and I'm proud of our relationship and what we have built together.

Choosing US

Being present over perfect, creating boundaries for our families, creating love that lasts, choosing collaboration over control, and living in our personal vision and values all put us in the right position to make daily choices that reflect our commitment to our families!!

Present Over Perfect

Put your phone away during quality time with your family. Turn off your notifications. Set a time limit on social media – and set an emotional filter! Remember that what you see is a highlight reel, and you should not be comparing yourself to anyone. Look for and try to create perfect *moments*, not a perfectly clean house, or a perfectly organized garage.

Family Boundaries

Say no more than you say yes. Stop overcommitting and over-scheduling your life (and your family's life). Remove unnecessary pressure for your kids to do more and achieve perfection. Delay decision making to give yourself an opportunity to say no for the right reasons. Be fiercely committed to creating "downtime" for your family.

Love That Lasts

Make sure that your marriage is your first priority – over any other relationship. Start making daily decisions to support that. Race to the back of the line when it comes to your spouse's needs. Schedule a date night. Commit to random acts of kindness. Learn your partner's love language – and then "speak" it to them daily. www.5lovelanguages.com Build trust and respect by being consistent.

Collaboration Over Control

Stop trying to control the people in your life and start collaborating with them to design the life of your dreams. Evaluate your capacity as a family, and if you have a capacity problem, build a plan to solve it. Become each other's biggest fan and supporter – working together for the common good of the family.

How We Do It Here

Determine who you are and what you stand for as a family. Identify your vision of the future and the values that define you. Create a framework to live in that keeps everyone healthy, happy, and moving in the right direction. Measure your success by your standards, not by anyone else's.

Choosing US is about the little daily decisions that deepen connections and create consistency.

Holly Hiding is so focused on people pleasing that she has a hard time saying no. As a result, her whole family is overcommitted. If Holly created a few boundaries, she could make space for individual passions bringing more peace and joy to her family. **Wally Workaholic** needs a framework that supports him in remembering to put the rocks in first – with family! Choosing to block time to build the most important relationships and to create love that lasts. Success at home always leads to greater success at work. **Polly Perfectionist** could change her relationships with her family by letting go of the idea that they have to be "perfect" and focusing on being present with them. Loving them right where they're at and making sure they know that we are all human and are allowed to miss the mark from time to time.

What decisions could you make today to deepen your connection with your family?

Are you gifting them the very best parts of yourself?

Embrace YOU – Focus on the power of being fully present with your family. Fiercely protect what you are building with boundaries. Say no to things that are good, so you can say yes to the best!

Design Your Life – Build a framework that nourishes your relationships. Make daily decisions that create a love that lasts. Evaluate capacity and adjust it for every season.

Build Your Legacy – Determine who you are and what you stand for as a family. Identify family values and create a vision that you can unify around. Develop a "safe space" for your family to live in authenticity.

It can seem overwhelming, but we really just need to focus on moving in the right direction. It is about connection and consistency with our families. Connection is the work of our hearts, we build consistency with our habits.

Your family's destiny is in your hands. Start working toward a common vision and make daily decisions that lead you toward that vision. Begin with the end in mind.

Chapter 4

SPIRITUAL FREEDOM

~

> "Our supreme duty is to advance
> toward freedom—
> physical, mental, and spiritual—and
> help others do the same."
>
> —Swami Vivekananda

Spiritual Freedom. Regardless of how you define it, you know how it feels when you experience it. Contentment, calm, joy, bliss, or peace. It is when we are able to live in the moment, and all seems right with the world. When we are able to exist absent of feelings of fear, anger, anxiety, or struggle. It is the state of being physically, mentally, and spiritually free.

Author Brene Brown provides a definition of spirituality for us in The Gifts of Imperfection:
"Spirituality is recognizing and celebrating that we are all inextricably connected to each other by a power greater than all of us, and that our connection to that power and to one another is grounded in love and compassion. Practicing spirituality brings a sense of perspective, meaning, and purpose to our lives."

So what are the practices that can bring us a sense of perspective, meaning, purpose, and the freedom that results? For some, it means seeking an inner god, worshiping nature, or acts of service. To others, it means contributing to the greater good, meditation, prayer or attending church. It is whatever practice moves us along a path toward the goal of spiritual freedom.

What if we could create a framework to bring more spiritual freedom into our lives? Stay in the moment more, and stop reliving the past or worrying about the future? And ultimately, help others to do the same. That is what this chapter is all about. The freedom that we feel in the deepest parts of our soul.

It is about the realization that we each have a purpose to serve and a gift to deliver. It is aligning our daily lives with our spiritual values. The realization that life is about so much more than just us. That there is something bigger and deeper to aspire to. It is awakening to the fact that our purpose is not found in trying to be everything to everyone. It is the journey toward becoming the best version of ourselves, so we can fulfill our unique purpose.

Once we discover and align with our purpose, we can stop the struggle and lean into surrender more. Setting ourselves free to live the life the universe has called us to fulfill. To stop worrying about what other people are doing, or what they think we should be doing. Remembering that all struggle comes from being out of alignment with our purpose or calling.

In the family chapter, we discussed saying "no" more, in this chapter, we are going to commit to saying "yes" more. "Yes" to life-giving and purpose aligning decisions. We are going to set fear aside and discredit the beliefs that we have allowed to limit our life.

What would happen if we operated within a framework that is faith-filled? If we were careful about what and who we allowed to influence us? What would our daily life look like then? We could save the best parts of us for the people whose presence in our lives move us closer to our purpose. Committed to how we personally stay faith-filled and how we help others do the same.

Let's explore what practices feed our souls, and how we can bring more of them into our lives. Every day, we have a limited amount of resources, including faith. Let's find the daily practices that can renew and restore that for us.

I don't know about you, but I'm ready to stop playing small and GO BIG. I want to live my purpose and dream big dreams. The dreams I was perfectly designed to pursue.

LETTING GO

A purpose-led life is what leads us to spiritual freedom. It is time to let go of who we think the world wants us to be, and step into *our unique* purpose. Discovering our calling and then surrendering to it. Moving past the struggle toward freedom.

Something Bigger

You know people who are clearly living out their life's purpose. You see it written all over them. They emit energy on a different frequency than everyone else. There are certainly well-known people we can refer to: Bill Gates and John Maxwell are just a couple who come to mind. It's obvious that they are living out their life's purpose. They fully utilize their unique talents and abilities. It brings them great joy and satisfaction, and it also allows them to contribute to the world what only they can.

We all have that potential. The potential to discover our purpose and fully lean into it. Surrendering to it, and to contribute what only we can to the world. There is a purpose each of us needs to fulfill while we are here, and it can be found in our innermost layer of authenticity. The work we did in the personal chapter should serve us well in this one. We need to dig a little deeper, though, and explore the calling that was placed on our lives from the very beginning.

It is uncovering who we are when we aren't trying to be who others need us to be. We often *lose ourselves* in serving others. The irony lies in the fact that we cannot serve at the highest level unless we are doing it from a place of purpose. When we are trying to be who we think others need us to be, we are actually robbing them of the best parts of us. The biggest and best gift we have to give only comes when we are in purpose.

We seem to spend the first half of our lives building a persona that we believe the world expects from us. Living in response to expectation keeps us from living out our purpose. Once we realize that, we can let go and begin the work of getting back to where it all began. Who we were from the beginning. Who the world *really* needs us to be.

Uncovering our purpose is a similar process to establishing our vision and values professionally. Our purpose goes deeper. It is in *who* we are, in our DNA, not *what* we do. It's our *calling*. It's why we are here.

Revealing Purpose:

What is your heart pulling you toward?
What are you doing when you feel that you are making the most significant contribution?
When do you feel the most alive?

What is worth devoting your life to? Your time, talent, resources?

The key to discovering our purpose lies in being open, present, and receptive to the answers to those questions. They can be indicators for you about our unique purpose. There may be a clue for you in the hobbies you love. Exploring areas of dissatisfaction in your life can give you some insight into what you are being called to solve.

You will know you are on the right path if it includes impacting others in some way. The key to an abundant life is not found in our lives – it is in what we bring to other's lives. Life is about people. We are here to connect. We may not be able to change the world, but we can certainly change our corner of it. We can change *somebody's* world. Someone or something hangs in the balance of our decision to uncover and embrace our purpose.

I'm still unpacking what it is for me, but I know at the core, it is serving others. That is when I get a rush of adrenaline and feel the most alive. When I feel like I am contributing in some way. Helping others move forward and grow. It is when I feel the deepest connections, almost as if our souls are intertwined in those moments.

You have more to offer the world than what you're offering right now. We all do. I am trying to uncover daily how I can stay more connected to who I am and why I am here. I want to answer the call. That is where I want to apply my time, effort, and energy in this season

Spend just a few minutes considering what your purpose might be for the season you are in. Maybe it is pouring love and faith into youth. Maybe it is mentoring, helping someone learn from your journey. Maybe it is providing safety and stability for someone who has none at the moment. Get still. Meditation, prayer, whatever works for you. Build some stillness into your life on a consistent basis.

If you become still enough, with consistency, and pay attention to what is in your heart, you'll eventually hear the calling.

When you seek your purpose, you will find that the universe conspires to answer and help you fulfill that purpose.

Surrender Over Struggle

I have good news and bad news.

Bad news first: At this point in my life, I am starting to recognize that we are the problem.

Have you ever:

- Experienced a co-worker who complains about everything, talks about everyone, and lives in a perpetual pity party? Have you ever made the mistake of joining them? It feels good, at first, to have a common enemy. Then you notice that you start to mirror their negative behaviors. Spending more time judging others, because it distracts from what is going on with you.

- Created pain for yourself and others based on flawed beliefs? Maybe you have made up a story in your head about how you have been wronged, and later learned that it was just a misunderstanding? Some people lose years out of their lives based on flawed beliefs.

- Tried to "fix" someone in your family because you were so worried about what other people would think? More concerned about appearances than whatever your loved one may be struggling through? Felt like your soul is more soaked in judgment than grace?

We are the common denominator in all of the drama, strife, pain, suffering, and difficult relationships in our lives.

Isn't that uplifting? Unfortunately, it is true. It would be great if we could blame it all on someone else – but the reality is – it's us. We are living exactly the life that we have designed for ourselves. It is either by default or design.

Good news: We are also the solution. We have the power to end the struggle and surrender to the lives that we were designed for. If you have been feeling more like a victim *of* your life recently, it's time to take control and create the life you have always wanted.

Wherever you go, there you are. If we're going to take ourselves on this journey with us (and I am not aware of any other way), let's take the very best version. We can make different decisions that move us away from that negative emotion and into peace and freedom. We can design a different path for ourselves.

We have all watched people who undermine their own happiness. We sometimes do it as well, it is just harder to recognize in ourselves. We create our own struggle, either by rehearsing something that has happened to us in the past or worrying about something that may or may not happen in the future.

When we rehearse how we have been wronged, we create more pain for ourselves by reliving it over and over again. We feel the weight of those emotions. We need to "tell our story," and garner support to justify our feelings. It keeps us stuck in a whirlwind of negativity. When we choose surrender over struggle – we release. Release means that we can come to terms with our emotions about the pain and move forward. It means that when we have said what we are going to say, we stop saying it. Sometimes it means forgiving others, and sometimes it is necessary to forgive ourselves. Either way, extending grace is the catalyst that helps us release. How much time are you spending rehearsing, and how much are energy are you investing in releasing?

The next time you have an emotional reaction to something, ask yourself this question: Where is my fingerprint on this? Often, a big emotional reaction comes up in us because we are actually frustrated/angry/disappointed in ourselves. It is painful to have to look in the mirror, so we look for someone else to point that emotion toward. The faster we can get to the mirror and weigh our role, the faster we can get past the pain and work toward moving forward.

Emotions are powerful indicators in our spiritual lives. Surrender starts by acknowledging them. When we can reflect on them, and process them in a healthy way, we can move toward peace and freedom.

Worry is the second component of struggle. When we are living in worry, we are missing the present moment. Worry reaches into tomorrow and brings it into today, robbing us from the present. Worry is always about the future, it is never in the moment. Worry makes everything bigger, more devastating than it really is. Faith reduces worry. If our faith is big enough, it will crowd worry out of our lives completely. We'll discuss building a framework for being faith-filled in just a bit. In the interim, reflect on what you are placing your faith in. Is that an area of your life that you need to strengthen?

We need to remember that it isn't the things that happen to and around us that cause us pain. It isn't even the things that might happen. It is how we *think* about those things. Every thought is either serving us, moving us deeper into our purpose, or distracting us from it. There is enough unavoidable pain in life without us creating more of it for ourselves and for others.

Surrender comes when we focus on what we have control over – ourselves and what we are contributing. Releasing everyone else in our lives (past or present) to their own journey. Letting go of worry and anxiety. Focusing more energy on discovering and living our purpose. More leaning in. Less rehearsing and more releasing.

Once we know who we are, we start to get clarity around what we should be doing. Building a framework of growth and continuous improvement for *ourselves* and keeping the focus on the work we need to do. Controlling what we have control over. Positioning ourselves to fulfill the purpose that only we can.

LIVING COURAGEOUSLY

Saying YES

When was the last time you said yes to something that made your heart race and your adrenaline rush? The universe is calling you to things that seem bigger than you can accomplish. That don't even seem possible. It may feel like you don't have the talent, the resources, or the education. But when you accept the calling in faith, things will happen for you that you could not make happen on your own. Doors will open that no person can shut.

In order to make space in your life for some big yeses, you might need to unravel some current obligations. If you are going to have the capacity to say yes to the right things, you are undoubtedly going to have to say no to some things that are not moving you closer to your purpose. I love how Sandra Stanley says it, "It's great having choices, but filling our days with all the things we *can* do crowds out time for the things we're *called* to do." I am saying no to some pretty good things these days, so I can create space to say yes to the best!

Here are some of my recent yeses that make my heart race and my adrenaline rush:

Serving on an Industry Board: In the last few years, I have served on a national board. Although I was incredibly honored to be invited, I was more intimidated. I knew the moment we prayed together before an industry presentation that our values and beliefs were perfectly aligned. I knew that I belonged here. That THIS is my tribe, and these are my people. If I had let fear rule my decision, I would have missed this. I would have missed all of the ways these people are enriching my life.

Writing this book: This book is very much a passion project for me. It is the result of a 5-year dream, and at this point, over 2 years of writing and rewriting. I originally set out to write it as an enhanced business card for my next season of life. It has turned into so much more than that for me, though. It has been a monumental growing and discovery process. There have been days of joy and jubilation and days of devastation and despair. I had to create a framework that helped me make the right daily decisions and remember that with everything in life – it is about consistency. Staying committed to the little things day in and day out, even when it felt like there was no progress.

Leading a Bible Study: Before we get out of this chapter, you will learn that I am a very faith-filled girl! I am not, however, a biblical scholar at any level. Regardless, when I heard the calling for *this* yes that scared me to death, I pushed myself out on that limb. I speak regularly and lead study groups professionally. I actually love doing those things. This feels different though, like there is so much more at stake. All of those fears start creeping in. Who am I to teach anyone about the bible? What do I have to contribute? I am not letting those fears stop me. I am leaning into them, feeling the fear, and doing it anyway.

All of those examples have included a journey far beyond what I have shared with you. A process of pushing past the fear and saying yes to the thing that scares me the most. I now evaluate fear differently in my decision-making process. The bigger the fear, the more likely it is that I will say yes. I know that is where all of the real growth is. It is on the other side of fear.

If you have some yeses you have been avoiding, try facing your fear by:

1. Imagining and accepting the worst thing that could happen.
2. Releasing your fear and anxiety about the worst possible outcome.
3. Becoming empowered to move forward in spite of the fear.

Every day we decide to do some things and not to do others. What is one decision you could make today that would put you on the path that was intended for you? One of the best gauges of spiritual maturity is the time between knowing (the calling) and doing (our obedience). I am trying to do everything I can to pay attention to the calling, and to shorten that gap.

Consider what big yes makes your heart race and your adrenaline rush. Find someone to share it with. Someone that will encourage to go out on that limb – that's where all of the really good stuff is. Don't let fear stop you from doing what you're called to do!

Becoming Faith Filled

Faith is believing that we are not alone. It is the belief that there is something bigger than our existence. It is allowing for the possibility that there is a divine order to everything. Divine order, meaning that the universe is calling to us and guiding us on our journey. That everything is actually in alignment and synchronized for our good.

So what, then, does it mean to be faith-*filled*? It means that in the depth of your soul, you believe and live into that divine order. You go with the flow of it so to speak, rather than trying to control everything. For some, their faith is wrapped in ritual. For some religion. Others derive their faith from nature or Mother Nature. Faith is the ability to trust what we cannot see. It is being willing to take risks and embrace the unseen.

When I think of faith-filled people, I am not necessarily referring to a particular religion or singular belief. I am referring to people that are obviously filled with faith. Faith that good ultimately wins over evil, and each of our lives is called to a purpose. You can see it written all over them, and you feel it when you are with them.

How then, do we become faith-filled? It starts with finding our tribe. A circle of people who believe in us and want the best for us. Who can pour into our lives in a way that takes us further *faster*? That keeps in check and on the right path. That brings out our best while also accepting our worst.

One of my most treasured mentors taught me 25 years ago that "your life will be the same 5 years from now except for the books that you read and the people that you meet." We're going to talk about the books that you read in the next section, this section is all about the people that you meet. People that can pull you closer to your purpose.

In John Maxwell's book, *The 21 Irrefutable Laws of Leadership, the Law of the Inner Circle*, he says it this way: The most rewarding inner circle can be your personal inner circle. Who do you share your heart with? Who knows your joys, sorrows, frustration, and victories? Who are your closest personal friends?

Make sure you include people in your circle who will also reel you in! People who will tell you (in love) what you need to stop doing.

For the different seasons we experience, having the right inner circle can literally save us. I witnessed that first-hand recently. I have a colleague who was struggling with alcoholism. He nearly lost his business, and more importantly, his family and entire life. I had a front row seat, watching someone who was in a life or death battle right before me. It was terrifying and heartbreaking.

One of my strongest beliefs is that we are here to love people. Not to judge them and not to fix them. I leaned into that belief and did everything

I could to "love him through it." I prayed for him every day. Thankfully, he was surrounded by many people who were doing that right along with me. He had a strong inner circle at a time when it mattered most. Fortunately, this is a story of redemption.

His faith journey had come to a dead end prior to his struggle with alcoholism. During the healing process, he had a personal experience with the Holy Spirit. An affirmation that changed everything. Now that he is healthy, he has returned to his faith, and is unpacking his purpose. Sometimes our struggles can be the very thing that strengthens our faith and positions us to serve. He has built a framework for himself that has led to healing. He prays as part of his morning and evening ritual. He attends Alcoholics Anonymous meetings daily. He sees a counselor weekly to continue to sort through what created the spiral and what will prevent another one. I used to tell him that there was a big, bold, beautiful life waiting for him on the other side of this. Now, I am watching him build it from scratch. I have so much respect and admiration for him and cannot wait to see what God has in store for his life. I know it is something big.

If your circle is not encouraging you, if it is not filled with people who want to see you win, then you need a new circle. Spend your time with people who can take you where you have never been before. With people who make you feel loved and who encourage you to live a great big, bold, faith-filled life!

BREAKING FREE

Feed Your Soul

What are the daily spiritual practices that feed your soul?

A daily spiritual practice refers to any ritual that we perform each day to quiet our minds and bring us into a state of peace or harmony with the universe and with ourselves.

We are going to review 5 categories of spiritual practices that we can leverage to feed our souls. They are movement, stillness, mindset, creative pursuits, and service. Each category has many possible practices, only a few of which are included here. It is up to each of us, individually, to determine what a spiritual practice is for us. It can be anything that helps us set our intention for how we show up in the world and deepen the connection we have with our own soul.

Movement

Movement of any kind can create an opportunity for healing, energizing, and calming, as well as contemplating. **Exercise** is one of my key spiritual practices. It can be anything from running to walking, to any kind of workout. Exercise can be a very freeing release of negative emotions or pent-up energy. **Yoga** is a great example that includes specific ways of breathing and moving that are often accompanied by visualization. **Dance** of any form is also a spiritual practice. There is something about dancing that connects us with flow and with our spirit. Especially when we let it come from the inside out, when we aren't worrying about how silly we look.

Stillness

We overfill our lives so that we can avoid the discomfort of reflection. It is in those moments of silence, when we don't really know what to do with ourselves, that we start to discover who we are. **Prayer** can be a powerful practice that helps us direct our mind and heart to whatever the Divine is to each of us. For me, that is to God. It's a conversation with Him filled with gratitude, devotion, and surrender. Prayer can be spoken or silent. **Meditation** is an exercise in silence that teaches you to control your attention. It can take us to a place where our minds are calmer and more focused. After meditation, I feel more positive, peaceful, and happy. **Camping** can also be considered a spiritual practice (see, I said it could be anything). There is something about the connection to nature and disconnect from the rest of the world. A level of stillness that settles and restores my soul.

Mindset

Controlling our mindset may be the most important spiritual practice. Remember the law of attraction? It is the belief that we can bring positive or negative experiences into our lives based on our thoughts. **Reading** books, articles, blogs, etc. that open our hearts and enrich our lives can be a very spiritual practice. I consider my daily devotional a critical piece. A daily reminder that my Creator has great plans for my life. **Watching** videos, TV, movies, etc. can either enhance or detract from our lives. There is nothing wrong with watching for pure entertainment, but we should select content that enriches our lives, attracting more positive than negative. **Visioning** generates the right mindset. Even if we don't use a formal vision board, we can picture what we want to attract into our lives. We can add affirmations to that visual practice. Never underestimate the power of the words that you speak to yourself.

Creative Pursuits

For many, a creative pursuit may be the most meaningful spiritual practice. **Gardening** can be more than a treasured hobby. It can become a spiritual practice as you create that sacred space that feeds life into your home. There is also a communal component to gardening. It might show up as a shared passion or a shared harvest. I believe this is a primary, spiritual practice for my dad. **Music** is a foundational spiritual practice for me. I love almost all kinds of music, but praise and worship music is a particular balancing point for me and an important part of my spiritual journey. **Cooking** can be a spiritual practice and is certainly one for my family. It is our collective love language. It is what we do. We prepare everything and cook together as a tribe, and those are the times I feel most connected with my family.

Service

There's a clear connection between people who serve and people who are happy. Serving can absolutely be a spiritual practice. **Caring** for others can improve our own physical and mental wellbeing when done in the right balance. The more love we extend, the more we find in our lives. **Teaching** others is a spiritual practice. I know that this is an area I have benefited from in my life. Often, the mentor gains just as much, or more, as the mentee. We should all spend more time pouring into other's lives. **Protecting** others reminds us of the call to acknowledge and respond to the suffering around us. Doing what we can with what we have. We can't acquire or consume our way to happiness, but we can *serve* our way there.

"Feed your soul by feeding the souls of others with love, kindness and compassion."

—Daniela Nikolova

We can determine the best way to feed our souls by considering what we can do to help feed the souls of those around us.

The possibilities of spiritual practice are limitless. It is all about each of us determining what it is that feeds our unique, individual soul, and weaving those things into our daily practices.

Stay open to the possibilities, amazing things happen on the other side of fear. Dare to try something new. Something scary, weird, or uncomfortable. Meditation was very hard for me at first, and now it is a refuge.

The daily choices we make are leading us somewhere. We become what we repeatedly do. We form habits, and habits form us. The question each of us needs to ask ourselves is, *are my daily choices leading me deeper into my purpose or away from it?* Let's spend some time considering what we want forming us.

Go BIG

Once we know what we are on this earth to accomplish, we must pursue that purpose diligently and without apology. Sometimes we shrink back from making too big an impact, fearful that it will make others feel insecure. The size of our dreams reveals the strength of our faith. Spiritual teacher and author Marianne Williamson encourages us to shine instead of "playing small:"

"Our deepest fear is not that we are inadequate. Our deepest fear is that we are powerful beyond measure. It is our light, not our darkness, that most frightens us. We ask ourselves, who am I to be brilliant, gorgeous, talented, and fabulous? Actually, who are you not to be? You are a child of God. Your playing small does not serve the world. There is nothing enlightened about shrinking so that other people won't feel insecure around you. We are all meant to shine, as children do. We were born to make manifest the glory of God that is within us. It is not just in some of us; it is in everyone. And as we let our own light shine, we unconsciously give others permission to do the same. As we are liberated from our own fear, our presence automatically liberates others."

We can be bold about our contributions to those around us without being egotistical or pushy. The key is to live in purpose with sincerity and enthusiasm.

God wants to inspire us to do something significant. Something big enough that it scares us. Something that requires faith. We need to move toward becoming who God intended us to be. It has been a lifelong journey for me with different purposes for different seasons. Dreaming big can be scary, but we need to remember that we are not alone. God will give us the strength and wisdom to make it happen if we call on Him.

Maybe it's time to stop talking and start doing. We just need to take the first/next step. When we are "in purpose," it ignites passion in the people around us. They start lining up to help us. Resources become available that we didn't notice before. We don't need a grand gesture or a giant leap, we just need to take that first step. Or the best next step. If we keep doing that, everything else will fall into place.

The value of a life will always be measured by how much of it was lived for others or given away. At the end of my life, I would like people to line up in appreciation because I've helped them be their very best, build their best life, or contributed in some way. We have to start now with the right daily intention. It is the little things done consistently over time that create our legacy.

Life is full of struggle, but it is our passion for our purpose that will carry us through the toughest of challenges. When we walk in our unique purpose, we collide with destiny.

Holly Hiding could discover her purpose by being truer to herself. Creating some daily spiritual practices like journaling and visioning could lead her deeper into authenticity and in alignment with her calling. **Wally Workaholic** could benefit from making space in his life for stillness. Creating a daily spiritual practice that creates reflection and reminds him that his worth comes from who he is, not what he does. **Polly Perfectionist** needs to create a spiritual journey that will lead her out of struggle and into surrender. Something as simple as the practice of daily affirmations could remind her that she is perfect just the way she is, with all of her imperfections.

What spiritual practices could move you closer to the life you want to lead?

Are you paying attention to the purpose the universe is calling you to?

Embrace YOU – Spend some time discovering your purpose and surrendering to it. Have faith that you already have everything you need to achieve everything you dream of.

Design Your Life – Invite the right people and daily practices into your life. Start by inviting one person to join you in your journey who can help you go farther faster, and identify one daily practice that makes sense for you today.

Build Your Legacy – Evaluate what you should be saying yes to. What would move you closer to your purpose? The choices we make today will determine the stories others will tell about us tomorrow.

Let's build a framework that keeps us in the present and out of rehearsing the past or worrying about the future. One that expands our faith and challenges us to a higher calling. One that creates more spiritual freedom for ourselves and for those around us.

Having a strong spiritual foundation positions us perfectly to fully live in what we believe.

Part 2

———————⌒———————

FINDING FREEDOM TO...

Chapter 5

LIVE WHAT YOU BELIEVE

―――――○―――――

"Your life is your statement to the world
representing your values, your beliefs,
your dreams."

―David Arenson

What is your life currently saying about you?
Does it reflect *your* values, beliefs, and dreams?

Living What You Believe starts with Embracing
YOU. It is living according to what *you* think and
believe. Identifying *your* personal values.
Resisting the temptation to live to the

expectation of others or conforming to *their* beliefs.

When we are living outside of them, trying to adapt to the expectations of others, we struggle. It brings an uneasiness that tells us that we are moving in the wrong direction. We sense that when our values, beliefs, and dreams are off track or out of sync.

When we are on track, we feel a sense of peace and purpose. It is clear to those around us. We are living fully into our values and personal beliefs and can start moving toward fulfilling our dreams.

This section of the book is where it all comes together:

Living What You Believe is built on the foundation of embracing YOU. Clarifying your values and beliefs. Owning authenticity.

Living in Purpose is a result of a designing a life that is purpose driven. Leveraging daily habits that keep you growing and moving toward your purpose.

Living Your Legacy is about creating a life of service today that will shape the story others tell about us tomorrow.

THEY ARE ALREADY THERE

Living what you believe is not as complicated or daunting as it may seem. There is no need to be overwhelmed or intimidated. It is primarily a discovery process. Resisting the pull to conform to what others believe and who they are, and leaning into what *you* believe and who *you* are. Building your list of beliefs over time as you recognize or uncover them. And then working to fully live into them daily.

It is as easy as one, two, three:

1. Start paying attention to what you believe. What hits you at your core?
2. Start a list of your beliefs, then consider categorizing them.
3. Review them often and make daily decisions that keep you *living into* them.

LIVING WHAT YOU BELIEVE

So far, we've discussed: Personal, Professional, Family, and Spiritual beliefs. It may make sense to use these categories or develop some of your own. Frameworks can be developed in any area of your life: Financial, Community, and Purpose-Driven missions, etc.

Once you start developing frameworks, and see how well they work, you may start applying this model to everything you do.

If you haven't downloaded the workbook, do that now at http://www.michellehubert.com/free-workbook. It includes a simple worksheet to get your personal values and beliefs down on paper. This one-page document will serve as a daily dashboard to living what you believe.

I have provided some ideas to get you started and help you along. Each of these areas has been represented in the book, and now it's up to you to define what is most meaningful in your life.

Personally:

- What we are contributing is more important than what we are receiving. If we stay focused on what we're contributing, the receiving part always takes care of itself.

- We attract into our lives what we think about. If we don't allow negativity into our lives and focus more on gratitude, we will get more of what we are grateful for.

- Be coachable and approachable. We teach people whether to give us feedback by the way we respond to it. Always thank others for caring enough to bring something to your attention. You'll teach them to be open and honest with you.

- Authenticity has no competition. The most successful and fulfilled people are those who are able to live in authenticity. Our greatest strength is leveraging our *unique* talents and abilities.

- I am enough, and what I contribute matters. I have nothing to prove, only a passion for serving.

Professionally:

- If you're not early, you're late. Show up on time, dressed, and ready to play, and you'll be in the top 20 percent. It really doesn't take that much to stand out in a good way.

- If we are not part of the solution, then we are part of the problem. If we recognize the problem, we must seek to be part of the solution.

- Five years from now, our lives will be the same except for the people we meet and the books we read. Our growth will come from who and what we fill our lives with.
- Who we learn from matters. Having a mentor that believes in us and sees more for our lives is critical to our growth.
- We are in control of our own personal and professional development. My growth and development are solely dependent on me and the daily choices I make.

With Family:

- Focusing on too many activities will keep us from the most important ones. Sometimes we have to say no to the good, so we can say yes to the best.
- Our contribution lies in being present, not in perfection. We need to focus on being present and the connections we are building.
- We don't sort the dirty laundry in the living room. Certain things are not meant to be said in public. Praise in public, correct in private.

- Show me your calendar, and I'll tell you what your priorities are. Make sure your relationships show up in your calendar.
- My job is to love them. Not to judge them or to fix them. Just to love them.
- It is about connection and consistency. Building connections with our hearts and consistency with our habits.

Spiritually:

- It's taking me a long time to become the person I want to be. When we know better, we do better. I'm on a mission to do better and to love better every day.
- Sometimes our journey calls for necessary endings. There are seasons in our lives for certain things, practices, and people. It is okay when it's time for a necessary ending that moves us into the next chapter.
- *True* freedom comes when we live according to our values and purpose. We struggle when we try to live according to what we believe others want from us. We live in freedom when we are true to what we believe, regardless of what others think or believe.

- If my relationship with God is primary, all my other relationships will flourish. In getting that one relationship right, I will have all the tools and resources I need to successfully navigate and nourish the rest.
- I am a human being, flawed and imperfect, but God perfectly designed me to serve the world in a way that only I can. It's in my imperfection that God has chosen me to serve.

As you start compiling your beliefs, pay attention to which ones come from within you and which ones have been impressed upon you. Living what you believe starts with knowing who *you* are. Embracing YOU. Grounding yourself in what *you* believe.

Getting them articulated will start to provide a new filter for your life. You will begin to reference them in daily decision making. Evaluating each decision as to whether it is in alignment with your beliefs. Moving forward with the assurance that you are growing deeper into authenticity, and into alignment with what you believe.

For me, it has been about clarifying what I believe in every area of my life and working daily to live into those beliefs. Although I have made progress, it is certainly not perfect. I tweak them a little each year. Different seasons bring discoveries of new beliefs. I am focusing on progress, paying attention, and pressing in one day at a time.

Living authentically and fully into what we believe paves the way to attract more people into our lives whose beliefs are in alignment with ours. It helps us find our tribe. Many people waste way too much time trying to be someone they aren't. I know, I wasted a lot of time trying to be someone who I thought those around me wanted or needed me to be. Here is the lesson: Never let who someone else is change who you are. Life is so much richer now that I now know authenticity is the only path to more freedom.

When I clarified my vision over 10 years ago, I had no way of knowing what my personal or professional life would look like today. But here I am, primarily living a life that's balanced, organized, and structured in a way that I can spend most of my time helping others, both professionally and personally.

That is possible because of the foundation I have in my organization and in my home. I know what I believe. I have built a framework on the foundation of my beliefs that sets me free to live authentically and in my purpose.

Embrace YOU

Embracing YOU is foundationally tied to discovering who you are and what you believe. It is the first step toward Living What you Believe.

In the PERSONAL chapter, we learned that it is about changing our thought process. Discovering our values and personal mission and live fully in who we are.

In the PROFESSIONAL chapter, we learned that it is about discovering or reconnecting with our professional vision and values. Being on a mission to serve our organizations and those who benefit from it. Leveraging our authenticity and unique talents to bring what only we can.

In the FAMILY chapter, we learned that it is about being fully present. Fiercely protecting what we are building with boundaries. Saying no to things that are good, so we can say yes to the best!

And finally, in the SPIRITUAL chapter, we spent some time discovering our purpose and surrendering to it. The importance of knowing that we already have everything we need to achieve our biggest dreams.

Embracing ourselves starts with knowing what we believe and then living into those beliefs in every area of our lives. Once we have that foundation to stand on, it allows us to start to design the life we want to live. Moving away from a life lived by default and into one that is purpose driven.

Clarifying our beliefs and leaning into them provides a springboard for us to take the next step. Fully living out our purpose.

Chapter 6

LIVE IN PURPOSE

---~---

"If you can't figure out your purpose,
figure out your passion. For your
passion will lead you right into your
purpose."

—Bishop T. D. Jakes

What fills your life with passion? Are you
leveraging that passion for fulfilling your
purpose?

As the quote states, our passions lead us to our
purpose. Things that bring us joy, fill us with

adrenaline, and break our hearts are indicators of purpose. They make our heart race and cause passion to rise up in us. They create a pull in our hearts that is so strong that we cannot ignore it. Paying attention to what those things are can help us live in purpose.

We all know what living without purpose looks like. We are going through the motions. Just barely getting by emotionally, spiritually, and financially. Surviving rather than thriving. We feel like victims, and everything feels like a struggle.

When we are living in purpose, we are passionate and energized. We feel an abundance of resources, both internally and externally, are working in our favor. There is a sense of passion and empowerment. We are so grounded that we are not distracted by road bumps or detours. We are *on a mission* every day to live as fully in our purpose as possible.

When we are living in purpose, it should be obvious to everyone around us.

MAKING SPACE FOR PURPOSE

It is about creating margin in our lives. That margin creates the freedom to live in purpose.

Designing our lives in a way that makes room for us to follow our passion. Creating a framework that pushes out chaos and makes room for more freedom.

We can create space for purpose in our lives in 3 areas:

Time: Create a framework and boundaries around your time that allow for decisions to live in purpose. Our capacity is limited, so we have to learn to say no to people and things that distract us from our purpose. When we are stretched to the limit, we have no time or energy left to devote to the pursuit of our purpose. In order to build love that lasts, we have to be sure that we are using our time to build connection and consistency into our lives. The activities and people that are truly important to us should be showing up in our calendars.

Talent: Overcommitting personally and professionally leaves us depleted. It is tempting to say yes to others who want to leverage our strengths. If that yes will move us deeper into our purpose, then we should consider it. If not, we should build an appropriate boundary, so we can utilize that valuable resource to serve our unique purpose. When we create space in our lives, we are able to fully utilize our unique talent to serve others.

Treasure: Too many of us are stretched to the limit financially. We overspend and under save. Living at the limit of our finances creates stress and chaos and does not leave room for a purpose-filled life. What can you start saying no to financially, so that you can say yes to something that moves you deeper into your purpose? In this season, I am so much more interested in life-giving experiences with my tribe, than with things. When we have no margin, we aren't able to generously give when we are called to do so.

Take some time to evaluate your framework for your time, talent, and treasure. Do you have space in these three areas to fully live into your purpose?

When we are able to live in purpose, it brings a whole new level of intention into our lives. Our purpose becomes part of our filter for decision making.

A great framework for living in purpose includes a few "go to" questions for decision making:

1. Will this move me closer to my purpose?
2. Will it distract me (or my resources) from my purpose?
3. How will it impact the most important people in my life?
4. How will it position me to better serve?
5. What will I have to give up to make space for this in my life?

Using this framework helps us filter our decision making. It helps us discern who we are trying to please and who we are willing to sacrifice. Let's make sure we are making decisions that serve those who are in our inner circle.

When we are able to live in purpose, it positions us to serve in a way that only we can. Refer to your workbook to help you create a framework that keeps you moving deeper into purpose daily http://www.michellehubert.com/free-workbook.

FREEDOM IN THE FRAMEWORK

Sometimes 'real' life shows up and disrupts our everyday living. A crisis can instantaneously surface in our careers, with our health, in our finances, or in our families. This is when having a strong framework makes all the difference. This is when we need it most. I suspect we have all experienced something in our lives that has stopped us in our tracks, even if momentarily.

Two years ago, my sister, Melissa, was diagnosed with tongue cancer when she was fifty-one years old.

Persistent ear pain, along with a bad fall that resulted in a broken nose and both arms, led us to an ENT specialist. It was there that we discovered that Melissa had a rare form of tongue cancer—adenoid cystic cancer—at the base of her tongue. Surgery was scheduled. We hoped they would remove the spot they had found, and we could get on with life. Unfortunately, due to the location and size of the spot, the surgeon had to make the decision to remove her entire tongue. A second surgeon took over and removed tissue from her right thigh to create a flap where her tongue had been.

Melissa came out of an eleven-hour surgery with an incision along her jawline from ear to ear. The incision on her thigh extended from her knee all the way up to her hip. She had a feeding tube and a tracheotomy. She had six drain tubes because of all the incisions. She had more than a hundred stitches along her jawline and more than a hundred fifty staples in her leg. It was horrific—a strong word, but appropriate. We were not prepared. I don't think anyone could ever be prepared for the journey we had ahead.

Melissa has been home for over a year and makes progress daily. She can now swallow and speak, and both are improving daily. She had her trichotomy removed recently, and the site is healing. Each step is a huge milestone. We celebrate every victory, no matter how insignificant it might seem. Every small step forward is monumental in a health diagnosis that is so complex and serious.

Melissa's doctors consider her to be in the top 10 percent of their patients in terms of resilience and positive attitude. She has been able to maintain her optimism most of the time. There were only a couple of days immediately after surgery that I could tell that she was feeling the weight of the situation and wondering what the future would look like. I could see the concern and fear in her eyes. She didn't stay in that place long, though, and I know that the pictures of her grandkids were what carried her through. Apart from those two days, no matter how hard it gets, she has always had a smile on her face and love in her heart.

When my sister needed me, I was able to live in my purpose. I was absent physically, mentally, and emotionally—in every way possible—from my organization and the rest of my family when she was recovering from surgery. My team was able to move forward within our framework, even though I was not present. I was perfectly positioned to use my time, talent, and treasure to serve her and my family.

I would not have been able to take time away to spend it with her if I had not established a strong framework in my life. I would not have been able to use my unique gift and experience to help coordinate her care.

What was breaking my heart at that moment was what she and our entire family was going through. As a reminder, my personal mission is to live a life that is balanced, organized, and structured in a way that allows me to spend the majority of my time helping others. The foundation that I had been building for over 10 years allowed me to live fully in my purpose at a time when it mattered most. There was definitely *freedom in the framework*!

I believe everything happens for a reason. I believe it's all by design, and that God had a purpose and a plan all along. I'm not sure why this particular cancer is part of her journey, but I know that she has been a very big inspiration to a lot of people, and that she will continue to be so in the future. She is a superhero to our friends and family, and her entire medical team. This crisis has brought our family together in a way that never would have otherwise happened.

Life is fragile. You do not know what challenges lie around the corner for yourself, or those closest to you. Build a framework for your life that allows you to live in purpose. Put yourself in a position to be able to go where and when you are called.

DESIGN YOUR LIFE

In the PERSONAL chapter, we worked to create a framework that supports the life you want to live. Bringing intention to your daily decisions so they align with and are reflected in your mission and values.

In the PROFESSIONAL chapter, we created a plan and processes that reflect your goals and dreams. We discussed utilizing your calendar to make sure you keep the main thing the main thing.

In the FAMILY chapter, we learned how to build a framework that nourishes our relationships. We discussed making daily decisions that will create love that lasts. And we learned to evaluate capacity regularly and adjust it for every season.

In the SPIRITUAL chapter, we reviewed the importance of inviting the right people and daily practices into our lives. Starting by inviting one person on your journey who can help you go further faster, and one daily practice that makes sense for you today.

If something is pulling at your heart, pay attention. Reduce the chaos and clutter in your life that keeps you from following your passion. Build a life and daily practices that positions you to live in purpose. Living out your purpose is the best gift you can give yourself and, ultimately, those closest to you.

Fully living into our purpose positions us to deliver our unique gift to the world in a way that only we can. It empowers us to build the big, bold life that we were each created for. Leaning into who we are and into our purpose puts us on the path to living our legacy.

Chapter 7

LIVE YOUR LEGACY

"Legacy is not what's left tomorrow
when you're gone.
It's what you give, create, impact, and
contribute today
while you're here that then happens to
live on."

—Rasheed Ogunlaru

What are you contributing today that will create
your legacy? Are you gifting your unique talent
to the world?

Living our legacy is about leveraging our purpose to make the contribution today that only we can make, one that lives on long after we are gone.

The lessons we learn from our parents and other influencers while we are young help establish the foundation of our legacies.

From my dad, I learned the importance of commitment and connection. Whether in his work, or in his personal life, he is known as someone you can count on. He lived out commitment in his career, rarely having missed a day of work or an opportunity to contribute at a higher level. It is also evident in the lifelong relationships that he still enjoys in every area of his life. Even after retirement, he has close friends from "work" that our entire family is blessed to know. Many of them have been a part of our lives for over 50 years. He works hard to stay connected to all of his family members, from great grandchildren to extended family. His legacy is the importance that commitment and connection play in our daily lives.

My mom taught me to have a servant's heart. We were (and still are) an "all are welcome" kind of a family. During my upbringing, it wasn't unusual to have "extras" around for a meal, and sometimes longer. She was always welcoming, and our home became a gathering spot for our friends. The diversity of our friendships was something she encouraged and supported. It taught me to create a home that radiates love and creates relationships. Her legacy is reflected in the number of people who were touched by her openheartedness.

My legacy is being shaped by the influence of both. I get my passion for commitment and connection from my dad, and my servant heart from my mom. As a result of their influence, my husband and I have built our home on the same foundation. We believe the more, the merrier. When our boys were at home, it wasn't unusual to have five extra kids around at any given time—and that was just the way we wanted it. We work hard to build connections with those around us. Hopefully, that is part of the legacy we are passing on to our boys, and they will live their lives with open hearts, committed to and building connections with those closest to them.

A lifetime of lessons and shared beliefs form the legacies we receive from our parents. It provides us with a foundation to build on. Living in what *we* believe, and fully in *our* purpose, positions us to live out the legacy we are trying to create every day.

BEGIN WITH THE END IN MIND

Have you heard of people going through the exercise of writing their own obituary? It can help us clarify how we would like to be remembered. By starting at the end point, we can start determining how we can bring living our legacy into our everyday decisions. It might be a little uncomfortable to think about what we would like people to say about us when we are gone, but it is definitely a worthwhile exercise. It can help us design a life that moves us in the direction of our choosing rather than leaving it to chance.

"When we think about the kind of person we want others to remember us for being, it's much easier to work backward from our deaths"
— Craig Groeschel

If we wanted others to say that we were kind, what would we have to do daily to cause them to feel that, and, ultimately, say it? If we would like to be known as generous, what daily decisions would we need to make to support that?

Consider the following questions:

1. What accomplishments personally and professionally would you want highlighted?
2. What would you want your family to say about you?
3. What stories would you want your friends to share about you?"
4. What would be missing from your community if you were gone tomorrow?
5. What would be said about your generosity with your time, talent, and treasure?

Clarifying the answers can help create a framework for living your legacy. Once you have the answers, you can start working to align your daily activities around them. To create the story that you want to be told and design the legacy you want to leave. Refer to your workbook and complete the worksheet to help you Live Your Legacy   http://www.michellehubert.com/free-workbook.

THE LEGACY I HOPE TO LEAVE

Personally

I hope my personal legacy is that I have lived authentically. Built a life steeped in my personal values. That I have spent my time with people who love well and whose beliefs align with mine. That we have been able to create space for each other in our lives, and to nurture the kind of relationships that are rare today. Something that goes much deeper than just day to day chatter, sharing the most authentic parts of ourselves and building a bond that connects our hearts.

I also hope that in some small way, I will have brought value to other people's lives. I hope that value is that they know that I love them and believe in them. That they know I will be here for them, no matter what. That they can count on me to celebrate with them, or pick up the pieces and find the courage to start again.

Professionally

Someone once asked me, if my colleagues were offered the choice of either receiving $10,000 or continuing to work with me, which would they choose? That's a powerful question that I've never forgotten. For a while, it kept me on a treadmill of trying to prove my worth. But now I'm learning that it is not about doing more, it is about doing more of the right things. The things that drive success for everyone around us.

My passion lies in developing others. My hope is that I have helped others find their passion and unleash it. That I have helped them discover a level of success and happiness that they never would have dreamed of on their own. Hopefully, I have been a good influence, helping others grow both professionally and personally.

With Family

When I think about legacy with family, I think about what I'm instilling in my boys. It's been said that an inheritance is what you leave *for* someone, and a legacy is reflective of what you leave *in* someone. It's the impact we have, not only on our children, but on generations to come. It's the values and culture that we pass down to them.

Hopefully, my legacy will be reflective of my love for them and for the values we reflect as a family. I hope my legacy is that they will become adults who contribute to the world in a big way. That they love freely and are always ready to contribute when needed. That they work to develop their own unique gifts and abilities and find ways to gift them to the world.

Spiritually

I am realizing in this season that it matters a whole lot less how "perfect" my life looks from the outside, and a whole lot more about who I am becoming on the inside. That how I look, where I live, and material possessions are not the treasures I seek. The filter that I will judge myself against is how I have made other people feel. Connection. Being better and doing better in that area. Bringing value to the most precious relationships in my life.

I hope my legacy spiritually is a faith that is so strong and bold that it is obvious to everyone around me. That I am so faith-filled that I am able to inspire others to join me on that journey. That I said no to things that did not move me closer to my purpose, and those nos left space for some pretty big yeses. That I pursued my purpose with curiosity and wonder and passion. That I got my relationship with my Heavenly Father right, and as a result, I got all of the rest of my relationships right.

"I do not want you to hear that I love you, but I want you to feel it without me having to say it."

—Khalil Gibran

Our legacies will be wrapped up not in what we do or say, but how we make others feel. They will be defined by how well we love. Connection and consistency will be the cornerstones. We need to pay attention to who and what we are building our lives around.

BUILD YOUR LEGACY

 In the PERSONAL chapter, we learned to leverage our values to help us focus on what we are contributing to those closest to us. We discussed the importance of delivering the best version of ourselves. Leading to a gift that will be unwrapped long after we are gone.

In the PROFESSIONAL chapter, we worked to discover the contribution that only you can make to your organization. We discussed the importance of staying focused on what we are contributing, rather than what we are receiving. Including exploring ways to mentor and develop others.

In the FAMILY chapter, we discussed determining who you are and what you stand for as a family. Identifying family values and creating a vision that you can unify around. Developing a framework that supports a "safe space" for your family to live in authenticity.

In the SPIRITUAL chapter, we started with evaluating what we should be saying yes to. Considering what would move us closer to our purpose. Setting intention in our lives based on the fact that the choices we make today will determine the stories others will tell about us tomorrow.

I am putting in the work every day to ensure that my influence will continue to resonate in the world long after I'm gone, and that the world will be a better place for my having been here. I hope that I will have lived up to my highest calling. That in the end, I made a worthy contribution. I don't think that is unique or revolutionary, I think it's what we all hope for.

"Your journey has molded you for your greater good. And it was exactly what it needed to be. Don't think that you've lost time. There is no short-cutting to life. It took each and every situation you have encountered to bring you to the now. And now is right on time."

—Asha Tyson

I know that my journey has molded me for the greater good, and I am grateful for every experience, especially the painful ones. I may not be successful at living my legacy just yet, but I am certainly making progress. Every day brings a new opportunity to have a positive impact on those around me. I am choosing daily decisions that will create the kind of legacy that I am dreaming about.

While it is true that we do not need to feel like we have lost time, we should have a sense of urgency in our lives. *Now is right on time.* Let's begin today. Let's not wake up one day and realize that time has passed us by and that we failed to create the lives we wanted to live.

GOING FURTHER, FASTER

As our time together moves closer to the ending than the beginning, it is my deepest hope that you have learned something or have been reminded of something that helps you along in your journey.

We have embarked on an expedition toward freedom. We devoted time to self-discovery. Uncovering who we are at our core, throwing off the façade of who we think others want or need us to be. Acknowledging our uniqueness and embracing the fact that we are each perfectly designed exactly as we are. Fully surrendering to our own authenticity.

Out of Chaos

Once we are on the journey, we will find more ways to bring that freedom into our daily lives. Setting the intention for our lives by living in what we believe. Designing our lives around living in purpose, and on purpose. Empowering ourselves to start living out our legacies. And of course, that will require more grace. We are human beings, and that fact will never change. We need to become comfortable with the fact that life is not perfect, nor are we. We need to stay focused on progress and away from evaluating ourselves based on the idea of perfection. Moving away from chaos and into purpose. Creating a framework for the life we dream of – one filled with freedom.

There has to be flexibility in our framework that allows for missteps and setbacks. There will be seasons of chaos. Those are the times when we need to rely on our framework the most, to keep us grounded and carry us through. We all encounter seasons of struggle due to financial, relational, emotional, or health challenges. The years we were raising our boys and I was traveling a lot were not perfect in any way. At times, they were pretty messy. Leaning on our framework kept us focused on the big picture.

The gift of imperfection is that it teaches us the necessity of learning to receive grace.

INTO PURPOSE

We were not created to merely survive, we were created to thrive. Our purpose is to give what only we can give. Everything that has occurred in our life, and that we have learned up until now has been in preparation for our purpose. Everything leading up to my sister's diagnosis was preparing me to live in purpose with her for that season. I learned to surrender my heart, and to focus on what was happening in the moment. That is a gift that I carry with me today. I am much more present in my everyday life.

What I have come to realize is that the stuff we accumulate and our professional accomplishments will carry no value in the end. When we leave this earth, we won't take anything with us, we'll be judged by what we leave behind. Our purpose is somehow intertwined with the people in our lives. It is the impact we have on them that will determine our legacy.

Our journey should not be difficult or complex. Less is more. We just need to take it one step at a time, identifying one tweak or nuisance in each area of our lives that, when implemented daily, will keep us on the right path. And when we get off course, we need to gently course correct back to where we belong. I am learning that every day brings a new opportunity to do better and be better.

In this final section of the book, I am going to share with you my plan for going further, faster. I am also going to introduce you to some resources that may be able to help you to the same thing.

WHEN YOU KNOW THE WAY, YOU CAN SHOW THE WAY

It starts with daily intention. Building a framework with seemingly small steps that, when accumulated, lead to freedom. It is like the practices of saving first or exercising daily. At first, it seems like nothing is happening. Then all of a sudden, you wake up one day, and everything is different. You are more in control. You are gaining ground. It is the intention day in and day out, little things done consistently over time.

It is my heart's passion to live a life that is balanced, organized, and structured in a way that I can spend the majority of my time serving others. I am living that out today and building a framework that keeps me in that passion for the long haul.

All of the striving, comparing, and controlling are the things that are keeping us bound. It is in the letting go, the surrendering, that we gain freedom. Surrendering to who we truly are and to the purpose we are called to. That is where the life we long for lives.

The journey to freedom is a lifelong endeavor that will be filled with discovery, acknowledgment, surrender, and grace. It starts with knowing and embracing who we are. It is the most tender part of the journey, and we need to be patient with ourselves. We need to extend grace and stay closer to our hearts than our heads.

You have everything you need, we all do. It was there before you started reading this book. I just reminded you of what you already know. Embrace You – Design Your Life – Build Your Legacy. Begin today. There is a big, bold, beautiful life waiting for you.

FREEDOM IMPACT GROUP

"And we know that in all things God
works for the good of those
who love Him, who have been called
according to His purpose."

—Romans 8:28, NIV

That is the Scripture that my two business partners and I have selected for the next chapter. Not the next chapter of this book, the next chapter of our lives.

For twenty-eight years, I have been blessed to love the work I do and the people I do it with. At the age of fifty, I am beginning to prepare for what the next chapter looks like for me: continuing to partner with people I love, doing work I love. Helping others find freedom, both personally and professionally. Continuing to sharpen and leverage my unique talents and abilities to help others go further, faster.

Some people are dreaming of filling their time with less work as they approach retirement. I am dreaming of more work—more *meaningful* work with those who seek freedom. Those who want to learn, grow, and get better, every day. I get to do that in my current career, but as I prepare for the next chapter, I am dreaming of doing even more of it.

We all need to think about what the next season looks like for us. How we will find fulfillment, and what we will be able to contribute to the world. Think about your own next chapter. Does it involve launching or working with a nonprofit? Maybe contributing to or volunteering for a cause you're passionate about? Is it starting a whole new adventure with a new business? Is it having the time to contribute to your family, maybe more time with kids or grandkids? Volunteering at school? It's important to consider what will bring you joy in the next chapter of your life.

I am partnering with two amazing people, and we are preparing to help individuals and organizations achieve leadership and operational excellence. Through Freedom Impact Group, we will be working hard to help others go further, faster. We have been called to that purpose and are building a framework to live it out in the next chapter of our lives. We are planning now for where we want to be ten years from now.

Our partnership was signed into existence on August 28, 2017, as a daily reminder of Romans 8:28, which appears at the beginning of this chapter. It is a reminder that God's plan is always better than our plan. He will be working for our good and for the good of others through us if we keep Him at the center of everything we do and put His purpose before our own. We are positioning ourselves to be able to leverage our extensive and diverse experience for the greater good.

Currently, we deliver the Operational and Leadership Excellence of Freedom Impact Group within our organizations and with a few select clients. In the future, we plan to have the capacity to make our offerings available to many.

Now that you've completed this book, you're already off and running on your journey to freedom:

1. Read Finding Freedom in a Framework (You can check this one off!).
2. Complete the assessment and worksheets – implement the ideas that resonate the most in your personal and professional life.
3. Apply those same principles to your organization.
4. Connect with us and STAY TUNED – we will keep you up to date on services Freedom Impact Group can provide as soon as they are available.

THE FOCUS OF FREEDOM IMPACT GROUP

We will be developing tools and resources that will help individuals and organizations go further, faster in 2 areas; Operational and Leadership Excellence.

We know clearly who we are and what we stand for and hope that your organization already has, or can gain, that same clarity. Defining your values and identifying a vision for the future is foundational. The next step is to analyze your current framework and processes, building and innovating them, creating a springboard toward operational excellence. Once that foundation is in place, it is time to invest in your biggest asset, your people. Making sure you have the right people in the right seat, and that everyone is growing will move you toward leadership excellence. With those 3 foundational pieces in place, you will be uniquely positioned for success.

Our organization lives by the mantra that there is "freedom in the framework." At our core, that is who we are and what we do. In the future, we will be helping organizations solidify their framework, creating more freedom; personally, professionally, with family, and spiritually.

If you believe we can help facilitate your journey for you, please visit our website at www.freedomimpactgroup.com. We will continue to update you on what we are doing in our current organizations and with our current client base. We will also share the tools and resources we love using. If you subscribe to our mailing list and be the first to be notified of updates from Freedom Impact Group including additional offerings, upcoming blogs, and other announcements.

Your next chapter will play out either by default or by design. Why not start today designing the next level of success for you and your organization, or the next season of your life?

OUR TEAM

Freedom Impact Group currently consists of 3 partners. Heidi Perez, Christina Roder and myself.

Heidi is the Chief Operating Officer of Mahaney Roofing, Design Build Construction, and Sheet Metal Inc. in Wichita, KS. She has held many leadership positions throughout her career. In her current role as Chief Operating Officer, she is responsible for organizational and leadership excellence at these three companies. She has trained many leaders and has implemented processes and systems in the areas of finance, sales and field operations that have led to exceptional growth and efficiencies in the organization. Process development along with growing and empowering leaders is her niche. She loves processes and systems, and has extensive expertise at building them. Heidi has a Bachelor's Degree in Psychology, a Master's Degree in Sports Management and is a John Maxwell certified speaker, trainer and coach.

Christina is the Vice President of Sales at Doextra CRM Solutions. She has vast experience building business units and leveraging systems and processes to drive success. Her passion lies in building our organization, Freedom Impact Group...and in helping you build yours. Her experience in starting new departments, managing budgets, strategic planning, marketing, leadership and sales consulting lends itself to driving business growth and success.

I am currently a Regional Vice President with Farm Bureau Financial Services. I have worked with the same company for 28 years and have loved every minute of it. I was a personal producer and business owner for 14 of those years, and I have been in a management position the balance of that time. In my everyday work, I help business owners achieve leadership and operational excellence. My deepest professional desire is to meet people and organizations where they are currently, and help them go further, faster, through operational and leadership excellence.

Our paths have crossed professionally in the past, and we have learned how to leverage our unique combination of expertise and experience for the greater good. The fact that we are all leaders in successful organizations, in addition to our work with Freedom Impact Group, puts us in a position to leverage our success to help your organization reach a new level of success.

If you feel that your organization is in alignment with our organization and would like to stay in touch, we hope you will reach out to us...we would love to connect with you!

Connect with us:
www.freedomimpactgroup.com

RECOMMENDED READING

Personal

- *The Secret* by Rhonda Byrne
- *Miracle Morning: The Not-So-Obvious Secret Guaranteed to Transform Your Life (Before 8AM)* by Hal Elrod
- *The Road Back to You: An Enneagram Journey to Self-Discovery* by Ian Morgan Cron

Professional

- *High Performance Habits: How Extraordinary People Become That Way* by Brendon Burchard
- *Traction: Get a Grip on Your Business* by Gino Wickman
- *The 15 Invaluable Laws of Growth* by John Maxwell

Family

- *The 5 Love Languages: The Secret to Love That Lasts* by Gary D. Chapman
- *Present Over Perfect: Leaving Behind Frantic for a Simpler, More Soulful Way of Living* by Shauna Niequist
- *Intentional Living: Choosing a Life That Matters* by John Maxwell

Spiritual

- *Divine Direction: 7 Decisions That Will Change Your Life* by Craig Groeschel
- *Chase the Lion: If Your Dream Doesn't Scare You, It's Too Small* by Mike Batterson
- *Falling Upward: A Spirituality for the Two Halves of Life* by Richard Rohr

GRATITUDE

There are so many people who have contributed to my life in so many ways. Some directly impacted this book, and some indirectly, but all influenced who I am and my journey.

Over the last 2 years, I have worked continuously and diligently to complete this book. There were times of great progress, and times of great frustration. Emotions ran the gamut from excited, exhilarated, and inspired to terrified, defeated, and complete despair. Sounds dramatic, doesn't it? That is the truth of this journey for me. It is the accomplishment to date that I am most proud of, mostly because of the perseverance it took to see it through.

That would not have happened without the support of some pretty amazing people, and I want to take just a minute to express my gratitude for their support and contribution.

FAMILY AND FRIENDS

First and foremost, to my husband, Tim. Thank you for believing in me from the day we met. For your unwavering support of my dreams, and for always encouraging me to *go for it*! Thank you for loving me unconditionally, just as I am, and for your contribution to our family. I can't wait to see what the next 25 years hold for us, I know it is going to be an amazing adventure!

To my boys, Cayle and Braydon. Thank you for your patience and grace as your dad and I learned how to be the best parents we could be for you. It would have been much easier for all of us if you had come with an "owner's manual" – or if we knew then what we know now. At this point, I think the best way for us to make it up to you is to be the best grandparents we can be for you someday. I'm so proud of both of you, and the men that you are becoming. Cayle, thank you for bringing Krista into our family, she makes us better, and I am not sure how we got that lucky.

Thanks to Mom and Dad for everything you have done my entire life to help me get to this point. Thanks for providing a safe and welcoming home for Melissa and me, and for instilling timeless Midwest values in us. Thanks to both of you for being such loving and supportive great-grandparents, and for the contribution you still make to both of our families. Mom, I wish you were still here to read this, but I know you are with us from your Heavenly home.

To my best friend and sister, Melissa. I am amazed by the combination of determination and grace you have displayed throughout this entire journey. I was stunned when you shared that you shed tears about your experience for the first time when reading this book. That is a reflection of your inner strength, attitude, and faith. I will forever be in awe of you, and I am still learning from you every day.

To all of my tribe...thank you. Thank you for all of the ways you have contributed to my life. I am grateful to be surrounded by people I love and that enrich my life in immeasurable ways.

MENTORS

To all of the mentors that have shaped my life, both personally and professionally, over the last 28 years.

There are 3 that have contributed in such a big way, that they deserve individual acknowledgment:

Garry Kinder, thank you for everything that you and your brother Jack have contributed to my life. Jack was the very first mentor who saw more in me than I could see in myself. He is the one that convinced me that I had everything I needed to achieve whatever level of success I dreamed of. And when Jack could no longer mentor me, you picked up where he left off. You have generously given of your time, talent and treasure to me and so many others. I will forever be grateful for our friendship.

Conk Buckley, thank you for pushing me to pursue this dream. Your presence in my life has impacted it in a way that is immeasurable. Thank you for always making sure that I am loving and leading well on the home front. For your interest and concern for the wellbeing of my family. I know this is not the book you encouraged me to write, but I promise, that one is on my to-do list. Thank you for leading by example and for making sure this dream became a reality.

Larry Riley, thank you for everything you have invested in me. You have had more influence on my professional growth than anyone in my career. Thank you for making it your mission to help me leverage my strengths and grow in areas of weakness. You taught me that I am in charge of my own professional development, and that it will be a priority if I make it one. I am grateful that you have continuously pushed me outside of my comfort zone and encouraged me to take on new challenges.

MY TEAM

First, thank you to my Farm Bureau Financial Services team who I get to work with every day. I always say that I love the work that I do and the people that I do it with. That's true, and I don't take that blessing for granted for a single minute. I am privileged to get to partner with each of you and thank you for all of the ways you have enhanced my life. For some of you, we have grown up together, and I will forever be grateful for the partnerships, experiences, and friendships. Here's to our continued success together.

Thank you to my Freedom Impact Group team, Heidi and Christina. The best years of my life professionally have been spent collaborating with you. You are both amazing women, and I couldn't imagine pursuing this dream with anyone else. Thank you for accepting me as I am, and at the same time, always encouraging me to reach for more. I love you both with all of my heart, and I can't wait to see what the next chapter holds for us.

Thank you to those who helped Freedom in a Framework come to fruition:

Libbye Morris, you helped me get my thoughts organized, categorized, and get the words on paper. You provided the structure I needed to keep progressing. Thank you for helping me take this step. I am so grateful for your support, keeping me on track and moving forward.

Patricia Wooster, thank you for helping me bring this book to life. Thank you for challenging me, pushing me, and for the growth you created in me. I am so grateful that you never allowed good enough to be good enough. Thank you for helping me through the publishing process and for always having my best interest at heart. Without your coaching, this book would not have been what it is today.

Morgan Chicchelly, thank you for helping me create and execute a launch plan to ensure more than just my family was exposed to this book! Your expertise in social media and marketing has been invaluable, and I am extremely grateful for our partnership.

Thank you to the authors in the Recommended Reading list, as they have each influenced me and my life in a powerful way. They have also unknowingly helped to shape my writing.

Finally, thanks to you. Thank you for purchasing my book and for bearing with a first-time author. It's really quite remarkable that you've hung on with me for this long. Let's not stop here, though, let's stay connected on Facebook, Twitter, email, or however you like to communicate. Our work together is just beginning, and I want to be able to be a resource for you in any way that I can.

Thank you from the bottom of my heart for taking interest in my book and for pursuing Freedom in a Framework.

ABOUT THE AUTHOR

Michelle Hubert, LUTCF, CLF is currently a Regional Vice President with Farm Bureau Financial Services and partner of Freedom Impact Group, LLC. Michelle is a long-time member of NAIFA and GAMA International and currently serves on the GAMA International Board. She has also earned an IASSC Certified Lean Six Sigma Green Belt™.

Michelle is also an independent certified coach, teacher, trainer, and speaker with the John Maxwell Team, and an EOS® Implementer. She has spent the last 28 years in the financial services industry helping business owners attain operational and leadership excellence.

She has found freedom living a life that is balanced, organized, and structured in a way that she can spend the majority of her time helping others. Serving individuals and businesses in this capacity has become her passion.

Today, Michelle and her husband, Tim, own and operate two local businesses in Oakley, Kansas, where they make their home and attend Gateway Church. Soon, they will be moving to Manhattan, KS where their two sons, Cayle and Braydon currently live.

You can reach Michelle at
michelle@freedomimpactgroup.com.